Fightnews.com®
Boxing Scorebook

Scoring a Professional Boxing Match

Scoring for professional boxing is done using a TEN POINT MUST SYSTEM where the judges must give the winner of a round 10 points, and the loser 9 points or fewer.

Judges are trained to score each round using the following scoring criteria:

1. Clean Punching (power versus quantity)
Who is landing the harder, more solid punches?
Who is hurting the opponent more?

2. Effective Aggressiveness
Is the fighter putting pressure getting the better of it?
Who is winning when the fighters exchange punches?

3. Ring Generalship
Who is imposing their will and style on the other fighter?
Who is making the other fighter do things they don't want to do?

4. Defense
Who is able to hit without being hit?
Who is demonstrating better dodging, ducking, blocking, parrying, ring movement and other defensive skills?

General Guidelines for the "10 Point Must System"

Judges should avoid scoring a round even (complete concentration and application of the scoring criteria will allow judges to pick the winner of each round).

The basic scoring concepts are:

• Round ends, no clear winner = 10-10 (discouraged)

• Close round/winning of the round by effective boxing = 10-9

• One knockdown and a winning of the round = 10-8

• No knockdowns, but a clear dominant winning of the round = 10-8

• Two knockdowns = 10-7

• More than two knockdowns = 10-6

• One knockdown and one point deduction to the same boxer = 10-8 (minus 1) = 10-7

• Two knockdowns and one point deduction to the same boxer = 10-7 (minus 1) = 10-6

• Boxer wins round, but has one point deduction = 10-9 (minus 1) = 9-9

• Boxer wins round, opponent has one point deduction = 10-9 (minus 1) = 10-8

Includes information from the Association of Boxing Commissions Regulatory Guidelines

Additional Rules

Incomplete or Partial Rounds

In the event that the bout is stopped in the middle of the round, the judges score ALL incomplete or partials rounds as if they were a complete round.

Knockdowns

Judges shall deduct points for knockdowns only when they are called as such by the referee.

Point Deductions

Judges may only deduct points for fouls when they are instructed to do so by the referee.

Source: Association of Boxing Commissions Regulatory Guidelines

Example Scorecard

FIGHTNEWS.COM® BOXING SCORECARD

BOXER NAME					BOXER NAME		
Amir Khan			VS		Lamont Peterson		
RUNNING TOTAL	POINTS DEDUCTED	ROUND SCORE	ROUND	ROUND SCORE	POINTS DEDUCTED	RUNNING TOTAL	
		10	1	8			
20		10	2	9		17	
29		9	3	10		27	
38		9	4	10		37	
48		10	5	9		46	
58		10	6	9		55	
66	-1	8	7	10		65	
75		9	8	10		75	
85		10	9	9		84	
94		9	10	10		94	
104		10	11	9		103	
113	-1	9	12	9		112	

TOTAL ⇒ | 113 | | 112 | **⇐ TOTAL**

WINNER: Lamont Peterson

OFFICIAL SCORES

112-113	112-113	115-110
JUDGE:	JUDGE:	JUDGE:
G. Hill	V. Dorsett	N. Vasquez

DATE:
December 10, 2011

CITY:
Washington DC

VENUE:
Convention Center

REFEREE:
Joe Cooper

WEIGHT DIVISION:
Super Lightweight

TITLE:
WBA, IBF world

NOTES:
Khan knocked down Peterson in round one...Khan deducted a point for pushing in round seven...Khan deducted ANOTHER point for pushing in round twelve!

FIGHTNEWS.COM® BOXING SCORECARD

BOXER NAME			VS			BOXER NAME		DATE:

RUNNING TOTAL	POINTS DEDUCTED	ROUND SCORE	ROUND	ROUND SCORE	POINTS DEDUCTED	RUNNING TOTAL
			1			
			2			
			3			
			4			
			5			
			6			
			7			
			8			
			9			
			10			
			11			
			12			

TOTAL ⇒ [   ] [   ] **⇐ TOTAL**

WINNER:

OFFICIAL SCORES

JUDGE:	JUDGE:	JUDGE:

DATE:

CITY:

VENUE:

REFEREE:

WEIGHT DIVISION:

TITLE:

NOTES:

Boxing judges are trained to score matches using the following criteria:

1. Clean punching (power versus quantity)
2. Effective aggressiveness
3. Ring generalship
4. Defense

Source: Association of Boxing Commissions Regulatory Guidelines

FIGHTNEWS.COM® BOXING SCORECARD

BOXER NAME   BOXER NAME

VS

RUNNING TOTAL	POINTS DEDUCTED	ROUND SCORE	ROUND	ROUND SCORE	POINTS DEDUCTED	RUNNING TOTAL
			1			
			2			
			3			
			4			
			5			
			6			
			7			
			8			
			9			
			10			
			11			
			12			

TOTAL ⇒ [ ] [ ] **⇐ TOTAL**

WINNER:

OFFICIAL SCORES

JUDGE:	JUDGE:	JUDGE:

DATE:

CITY:

VENUE:

REFEREE:

WEIGHT DIVISION:

TITLE:

NOTES:

Boxing judges are trained to score matches using the following criteria:

1. Clean punching (power versus quantity)
2. Effective aggressiveness
3. Ring generalship
4. Defense

Source: Association of Boxing Commissions Regulatory Guidelines

FIGHTNEWS.COM® BOXING SCORECARD

BOXER NAME   BOXER NAME

VS

RUNNING TOTAL	POINTS DEDUCTED	ROUND SCORE	ROUND	ROUND SCORE	POINTS DEDUCTED	RUNNING TOTAL
			1			
			2			
			3			
			4			
			5			
			6			
			7			
			8			
			9			
			10			
			11			
			12			

TOTAL ⇒   **⇐ TOTAL**

WINNER:

OFFICIAL SCORES

JUDGE:	JUDGE:	JUDGE:

DATE:

CITY:

VENUE:

REFEREE:

WEIGHT DIVISION:

TITLE:

NOTES:

Boxing judges are trained to score matches using the following criteria:

1. Clean punching (power versus quantity)
2. Effective aggressiveness
3. Ring generalship
4. Defense

Source: Association of Boxing Commissions Regulatory Guidelines

FIGHTNEWS.COM® BOXING SCORECARD

BOXER NAME			VS		BOXER NAME		

RUNNING TOTAL	POINTS DEDUCTED	ROUND SCORE	ROUND	ROUND SCORE	POINTS DEDUCTED	RUNNING TOTAL
			1			
			2			
			3			
			4			
			5			
			6			
			7			
			8			
			9			
			10			
			11			
			12			

TOTAL ⇒ [ ] [ ] **⇐ TOTAL**

WINNER:

OFFICIAL SCORES

JUDGE:	JUDGE:	JUDGE:

DATE:

CITY:

VENUE:

REFEREE:

WEIGHT DIVISION:

TITLE:

NOTES:

Boxing judges are trained to score matches using the following criteria:

1. Clean punching (power versus quantity)
2. Effective aggressiveness
3. Ring generalship
4. Defense

Source: Association of Boxing Commissions Regulatory Guidelines

FIGHTNEWS.COM® BOXING SCORECARD

BOXER NAME   BOXER NAME

VS

RUNNING TOTAL	POINTS DEDUCTED	ROUND SCORE	ROUND	ROUND SCORE	POINTS DEDUCTED	RUNNING TOTAL
			1			
			2			
			3			
			4			
			5			
			6			
			7			
			8			
			9			
			10			
			11			
			12			

TOTAL ⇒   **⇐ TOTAL**

WINNER:

OFFICIAL SCORES

JUDGE:	JUDGE:	JUDGE:

DATE:

CITY:

VENUE:

REFEREE:

WEIGHT DIVISION:

TITLE:

NOTES:

Boxing judges are trained to score matches using the following criteria:

1. Clean punching (power versus quantity)
2. Effective aggressiveness
3. Ring generalship
4. Defense

Source: Association of Boxing Commissions Regulatory Guidelines

FIGHTNEWS.COM® BOXING SCORECARD

BOXER NAME   BOXER NAME

VS

RUNNING TOTAL	POINTS DEDUCTED	ROUND SCORE	ROUND	ROUND SCORE	POINTS DEDUCTED	RUNNING TOTAL
			1			
			2			
			3			
			4			
			5			
			6			
			7			
			8			
			9			
			10			
			11			
			12			

TOTAL ⇒   **⇐ TOTAL**

WINNER:

OFFICIAL SCORES

JUDGE:	JUDGE:	JUDGE:

DATE:

CITY:

VENUE:

REFEREE:

WEIGHT DIVISION:

TITLE:

NOTES:

Boxing judges are trained to score matches using the following criteria:

1. Clean punching (power versus quantity)
2. Effective aggressiveness
3. Ring generalship
4. Defense

Source: Association of Boxing Commissions Regulatory Guidelines

FIGHTNEWS.COM® BOXING SCORECARD

BOXER NAME				BOXER NAME		
			VS			

RUNNING TOTAL	POINTS DEDUCTED	ROUND SCORE	ROUND	ROUND SCORE	POINTS DEDUCTED	RUNNING TOTAL
			1			
			2			
			3			
			4			
			5			
			6			
			7			
			8			
			9			
			10			
			11			
			12			

TOTAL ⇒ [ ] [ ] **⇐ TOTAL**

DATE:

CITY:

VENUE:

REFEREE:

WEIGHT DIVISION:

TITLE:

NOTES:

WINNER:

OFFICIAL SCORES

JUDGE:	JUDGE:	JUDGE:

Boxing judges are trained to score matches using the following criteria:

1. Clean punching (power versus quantity)
2. Effective aggressiveness
3. Ring generalship
4. Defense

Source: Association of Boxing Commissions Regulatory Guidelines

FIGHTNEWS.COM® BOXING SCORECARD

	BOXER NAME		VS		BOXER NAME		DATE:

RUNNING TOTAL	POINTS DEDUCTED	ROUND SCORE	ROUND	ROUND SCORE	POINTS DEDUCTED	RUNNING TOTAL
			1			
			2			
			3			
			4			
			5			
			6			
			7			
			8			
			9			
			10			
			11			
			12			

TOTAL ⟹ [ ] [ ] **⟸ TOTAL**

WINNER:

DATE:

CITY:

VENUE:

REFEREE:

WEIGHT DIVISION:

TITLE:

NOTES:

OFFICIAL SCORES

JUDGE:	JUDGE:	JUDGE:

Boxing judges are trained to score matches using the following criteria:

1. Clean punching (power versus quantity)
2. Effective aggressiveness
3. Ring generalship
4. Defense

Source: Association of Boxing Commissions Regulatory Guidelines

FIGHTNEWS.COM® BOXING SCORECARD

BOXER NAME			VS		BOXER NAME		DATE:

RUNNING TOTAL	POINTS DEDUCTED	ROUND SCORE	ROUND	ROUND SCORE	POINTS DEDUCTED	RUNNING TOTAL
			1			
			2			
			3			
			4			
			5			
			6			
			7			
			8			
			9			
			10			
			11			
			12			

CITY:

VENUE:

REFEREE:

WEIGHT DIVISION:

TITLE:

NOTES:

TOTAL ⇒ [ ] [ ] **⇐ TOTAL**

WINNER:

OFFICIAL SCORES

JUDGE:	JUDGE:	JUDGE:

Boxing judges are trained to score matches using the following criteria:

1. Clean punching (power versus quantity)
2. Effective aggressiveness
3. Ring generalship
4. Defense

Source: Association of Boxing Commissions Regulatory Guidelines

FIGHTNEWS.COM® BOXING SCORECARD

BOXER NAME			VS		BOXER NAME	

RUNNING TOTAL	POINTS DEDUCTED	ROUND SCORE	ROUND	ROUND SCORE	POINTS DEDUCTED	RUNNING TOTAL
			1			
			2			
			3			
			4			
			5			
			6			
			7			
			8			
			9			
			10			
			11			
			12			

TOTAL ⇒ [   ] [   ] **⇐ TOTAL**

WINNER:

OFFICIAL SCORES

JUDGE:	JUDGE:	JUDGE:

DATE:

CITY:

VENUE:

REFEREE:

WEIGHT DIVISION:

TITLE:

NOTES:

Boxing judges are trained to score matches using the following criteria:

1. Clean punching (power versus quantity)
2. Effective aggressiveness
3. Ring generalship
4. Defense

Source: Association of Boxing Commissions Regulatory Guidelines

FIGHTNEWS.COM® BOXING SCORECARD

BOXER NAME			VS		BOXER NAME	

RUNNING TOTAL	POINTS DEDUCTED	ROUND SCORE	ROUND	ROUND SCORE	POINTS DEDUCTED	RUNNING TOTAL
			1			
			2			
			3			
			4			
			5			
			6			
			7			
			8			
			9			
			10			
			11			
			12			

TOTAL ⟹ [ ] [ ] **⟸ TOTAL**

WINNER:

OFFICIAL SCORES

JUDGE:	JUDGE:	JUDGE:

DATE:

CITY:

VENUE:

REFEREE:

WEIGHT DIVISION:

TITLE:

NOTES:

Boxing judges are trained to score matches using the following criteria:

1. Clean punching (power versus quantity)
2. Effective aggressiveness
3. Ring generalship
4. Defense

Source: Association of Boxing Commissions Regulatory Guidelines

FIGHTNEWS.COM® BOXING SCORECARD

BOXER NAME			VS		BOXER NAME	

RUNNING TOTAL	POINTS DEDUCTED	ROUND SCORE	ROUND	ROUND SCORE	POINTS DEDUCTED	RUNNING TOTAL
			1			
			2			
			3			
			4			
			5			
			6			
			7			
			8			
			9			
			10			
			11			
			12			

TOTAL ⇒ [ ] [ ] **⇐ TOTAL**

WINNER:

OFFICIAL SCORES

JUDGE:	JUDGE:	JUDGE:

DATE:

CITY:

VENUE:

REFEREE:

WEIGHT DIVISION:

TITLE:

NOTES:

Boxing judges are trained to score matches using the following criteria:

1. Clean punching (power versus quantity)
2. Effective aggressiveness
3. Ring generalship
4. Defense

Source: Association of Boxing Commissions Regulatory Guidelines

FIGHTNEWS.COM® BOXING SCORECARD

BOXER NAME		VS			BOXER NAME		DATE:

RUNNING TOTAL	POINTS DEDUCTED	ROUND SCORE	ROUND	ROUND SCORE	POINTS DEDUCTED	RUNNING TOTAL
			1			
			2			
			3			
			4			
			5			
			6			
			7			
			8			
			9			
			10			
			11			
			12			

TOTAL ⇒ [   ] [   ] **⇐ TOTAL**

WINNER:

OFFICIAL SCORES

JUDGE:	JUDGE:	JUDGE:

DATE:

CITY:

VENUE:

REFEREE:

WEIGHT DIVISION:

TITLE:

NOTES:

Boxing judges are trained to score matches using the following criteria:

1. Clean punching (power versus quantity)
2. Effective aggressiveness
3. Ring generalship
4. Defense

Source: Association of Boxing Commissions Regulatory Guidelines

FIGHTNEWS.COM® BOXING SCORECARD

BOXER NAME							
			VS		BOXER NAME		
RUNNING TOTAL	POINTS DEDUCTED	ROUND SCORE	ROUND	ROUND SCORE	POINTS DEDUCTED	RUNNING TOTAL
			1			
			2			
			3			
			4			
			5			
			6			
			7			
			8			
			9			
			10			
			11			
			12			

TOTAL ⇒ [ ] [ ] **⇐ TOTAL**

WINNER:

OFFICIAL SCORES

JUDGE:	JUDGE:	JUDGE:

DATE:
CITY:
VENUE:
REFEREE:
WEIGHT DIVISION:
TITLE:
NOTES:

Boxing judges are trained to score matches using the following criteria:

1. Clean punching (power versus quantity)
2. Effective aggressiveness
3. Ring generalship
4. Defense

Source: Association of Boxing Commissions Regulatory Guidelines

FIGHTNEWS.COM® BOXING SCORECARD

BOXER NAME   BOXER NAME

VS

RUNNING TOTAL	POINTS DEDUCTED	ROUND SCORE	ROUND	ROUND SCORE	POINTS DEDUCTED	RUNNING TOTAL
			1			
			2			
			3			
			4			
			5			
			6			
			7			
			8			
			9			
			10			
			11			
			12			

TOTAL ⇒ [ ] [ ] **⇐ TOTAL**

WINNER:

OFFICIAL SCORES

JUDGE:	JUDGE:	JUDGE:

DATE:

CITY:

VENUE:

REFEREE:

WEIGHT DIVISION:

TITLE:

NOTES:

Boxing judges are trained to score matches using the following criteria:

1. Clean punching (power versus quantity)
2. Effective aggressiveness
3. Ring generalship
4. Defense

Source: Association of Boxing Commissions Regulatory Guidelines

FIGHTNEWS.COM® BOXING SCORECARD

BOXER NAME						BOXER NAME	
			VS				

RUNNING TOTAL	POINTS DEDUCTED	ROUND SCORE	ROUND	ROUND SCORE	POINTS DEDUCTED	RUNNING TOTAL
			1			
			2			
			3			
			4			
			5			
			6			
			7			
			8			
			9			
			10			
			11			
			12			

TOTAL ⇒ | | **⇐ TOTAL**

WINNER:

OFFICIAL SCORES

JUDGE:	JUDGE:	JUDGE:

DATE:

CITY:

VENUE:

REFEREE:

WEIGHT DIVISION:

TITLE:

NOTES:

Boxing judges are trained to score matches using the following criteria:

1. Clean punching (power versus quantity)
2. Effective aggressiveness
3. Ring generalship
4. Defense

Source: Association of Boxing Commissions Regulatory Guidelines

FIGHTNEWS.COM® BOXING SCORECARD

BOXER NAME   BOXER NAME

VS

RUNNING TOTAL	POINTS DEDUCTED	ROUND SCORE	ROUND	ROUND SCORE	POINTS DEDUCTED	RUNNING TOTAL
			1			
			2			
			3			
			4			
			5			
			6			
			7			
			8			
			9			
			10			
			11			
			12			

TOTAL ⇒ [ ] [ ] **⇐ TOTAL**

WINNER:

OFFICIAL SCORES

JUDGE:	JUDGE:	JUDGE:

DATE:

CITY:

VENUE:

REFEREE:

WEIGHT DIVISION:

TITLE:

NOTES:

Boxing judges are trained to score matches using the following criteria:

1. Clean punching (power versus quantity)
2. Effective aggressiveness
3. Ring generalship
4. Defense

Source: Association of Boxing Commissions Regulatory Guidelines

FIGHTNEWS.COM® BOXING SCORECARD

BOXER NAME | BOXER NAME | DATE:

VS

RUNNING TOTAL	POINTS DEDUCTED	ROUND SCORE	ROUND	ROUND SCORE	POINTS DEDUCTED	RUNNING TOTAL
			1			
			2			
			3			
			4			
			5			
			6			
			7			
			8			
			9			
			10			
			11			
			12			

TOTAL ⇒   **⇐ TOTAL**

WINNER:

OFFICIAL SCORES

JUDGE:	JUDGE:	JUDGE:

CITY:

VENUE:

REFEREE:

WEIGHT DIVISION:

TITLE:

NOTES:

Boxing judges are trained to score matches using the following criteria:

1. Clean punching (power versus quantity)
2. Effective aggressiveness
3. Ring generalship
4. Defense

Source: Association of Boxing Commissions Regulatory Guidelines

FIGHTNEWS.COM® BOXING SCORECARD

| BOXER NAME | | | | | | | DATE: |
| VS | | | | | | | CITY: |

RUNNING TOTAL	POINTS DEDUCTED	ROUND SCORE	ROUND	ROUND SCORE	POINTS DEDUCTED	RUNNING TOTAL
			1			
			2			
			3			
			4			
			5			
			6			
			7			
			8			
			9			
			10			
			11			
			12			

VENUE:

REFEREE:

WEIGHT DIVISION:

TITLE:

NOTES:

TOTAL ⇒ [ ] [ ] **⇐ TOTAL**

WINNER:

OFFICIAL SCORES

JUDGE:	JUDGE:	JUDGE:

Boxing judges are trained to score matches using the following criteria:

1. Clean punching (power versus quantity)
2. Effective aggressiveness
3. Ring generalship
4. Defense

Source: Association of Boxing Commissions Regulatory Guidelines

FIGHTNEWS.COM® BOXING SCORECARD

BOXER NAME   BOXER NAME

<u>VS</u>

RUNNING TOTAL	POINTS DEDUCTED	ROUND SCORE	ROUND	ROUND SCORE	POINTS DEDUCTED	RUNNING TOTAL
			1			
			2			
			3			
			4			
			5			
			6			
			7			
			8			
			9			
			10			
			11			
			12			

TOTAL ⇒ [ ] [ ] **⇐ TOTAL**

WINNER:

OFFICIAL SCORES

JUDGE:	JUDGE:	JUDGE:

DATE:

CITY:

VENUE:

REFEREE:

WEIGHT DIVISION:

TITLE:

NOTES:

Boxing judges are trained to score matches using the following criteria:

1. Clean punching (power versus quantity)
2. Effective aggressiveness
3. Ring generalship
4. Defense

Source: Association of Boxing Commissions Regulatory Guidelines

FIGHTNEWS.COM® BOXING SCORECARD

BOXER NAME			VS		BOXER NAME		DATE:

RUNNING TOTAL	POINTS DEDUCTED	ROUND SCORE	ROUND	ROUND SCORE	POINTS DEDUCTED	RUNNING TOTAL
			1			
			2			
			3			
			4			
			5			
			6			
			7			
			8			
			9			
			10			
			11			
			12			

TOTAL ⇒ [   ] [   ] **⇐ TOTAL**

DATE:

CITY:

VENUE:

REFEREE:

WEIGHT DIVISION:

TITLE:

NOTES:

WINNER:

OFFICIAL SCORES

JUDGE:	JUDGE:	JUDGE:

Boxing judges are trained to score matches using the following criteria:

1. Clean punching (power versus quantity)
2. Effective aggressiveness
3. Ring generalship
4. Defense

Source: Association of Boxing Commissions Regulatory Guidelines

FIGHTNEWS.COM® BOXING SCORECARD

BOXER NAME			VS		BOXER NAME			DATE:

RUNNING TOTAL	POINTS DEDUCTED	ROUND SCORE	ROUND	ROUND SCORE	POINTS DEDUCTED	RUNNING TOTAL
			1			
			2			
			3			
			4			
			5			
			6			
			7			
			8			
			9			
			10			
			11			
			12			

TOTAL ⇒ [ ] [ ] **⇐ TOTAL**

DATE:

CITY:

VENUE:

REFEREE:

WEIGHT DIVISION:

TITLE:

NOTES:

WINNER:

OFFICIAL SCORES

JUDGE:	JUDGE:	JUDGE:

Boxing judges are trained to score matches using the following criteria:

1. Clean punching (power versus quantity)
2. Effective aggressiveness
3. Ring generalship
4. Defense

Source: Association of Boxing Commissions Regulatory Guidelines

FIGHTNEWS.COM® BOXING SCORECARD

BOXER NAME						BOXER NAME	

VS

RUNNING TOTAL	POINTS DEDUCTED	ROUND SCORE	ROUND	ROUND SCORE	POINTS DEDUCTED	RUNNING TOTAL
			1			
			2			
			3			
			4			
			5			
			6			
			7			
			8			
			9			
			10			
			11			
			12			

TOTAL ⇒ | | **⇐ TOTAL**

WINNER:

OFFICIAL SCORES

JUDGE:	JUDGE:	JUDGE:

DATE:

CITY:

VENUE:

REFEREE:

WEIGHT DIVISION:

TITLE:

NOTES:

Boxing judges are trained to score matches using the following criteria:

1. Clean punching (power versus quantity)
2. Effective aggressiveness
3. Ring generalship
4. Defense

Source: Association of Boxing Commissions Regulatory Guidelines

FIGHTNEWS.COM® BOXING SCORECARD

BOXER NAME   BOXER NAME

VS

RUNNING TOTAL	POINTS DEDUCTED	ROUND SCORE	ROUND	ROUND SCORE	POINTS DEDUCTED	RUNNING TOTAL
			1			
			2			
			3			
			4			
			5			
			6			
			7			
			8			
			9			
			10			
			11			
			12			

TOTAL ⇒   **⇐ TOTAL**

WINNER:

OFFICIAL SCORES

JUDGE:	JUDGE:	JUDGE:

DATE:

CITY:

VENUE:

REFEREE:

WEIGHT DIVISION:

TITLE:

NOTES:

Boxing judges are trained to score matches using the following criteria:

1. Clean punching (power versus quantity)
2. Effective aggressiveness
3. Ring generalship
4. Defense

Source: Association of Boxing Commissions Regulatory Guidelines

FIGHTNEWS.COM® BOXING SCORECARD

BOXER NAME					BOXER NAME			DATE:
			VS					

RUNNING TOTAL	POINTS DEDUCTED	ROUND SCORE	ROUND	ROUND SCORE	POINTS DEDUCTED	RUNNING TOTAL
			1			
			2			
			3			
			4			
			5			
			6			
			7			
			8			
			9			
			10			
			11			
			12			

TOTAL ⇒ [   ] [   ] **⇐ TOTAL**

DATE:	
CITY:	
VENUE:	
REFEREE:	
WEIGHT DIVISION:	
TITLE:	
NOTES:	

WINNER:

OFFICIAL SCORES

JUDGE:	JUDGE:	JUDGE:

Boxing judges are trained to score matches using the following criteria:

1. Clean punching (power versus quantity)
2. Effective aggressiveness
3. Ring generalship
4. Defense

Source: Association of Boxing Commissions Regulatory Guidelines

FIGHTNEWS.COM® BOXING SCORECARD

BOXER NAME   BOXER NAME

VS

RUNNING TOTAL	POINTS DEDUCTED	ROUND SCORE	ROUND	ROUND SCORE	POINTS DEDUCTED	RUNNING TOTAL
			1			
			2			
			3			
			4			
			5			
			6			
			7			
			8			
			9			
			10			
			11			
			12			

TOTAL ⇒   **⇐ TOTAL**

WINNER:

OFFICIAL SCORES

JUDGE: JUDGE: JUDGE:

DATE:

CITY:

VENUE:

REFEREE:

WEIGHT DIVISION:

TITLE:

NOTES:

Boxing judges are trained to score matches using the following criteria:

1. Clean punching (power versus quantity)
2. Effective aggressiveness
3. Ring generalship
4. Defense

Source: Association of Boxing Commissions Regulatory Guidelines

FIGHTNEWS.COM® BOXING SCORECARD

BOXER NAME   BOXER NAME

VS

RUNNING TOTAL	POINTS DEDUCTED	ROUND SCORE	ROUND	ROUND SCORE	POINTS DEDUCTED	RUNNING TOTAL
			1			
			2			
			3			
			4			
			5			
			6			
			7			
			8			
			9			
			10			
			11			
			12			

TOTAL ⇒ [   ] [   ] **⇐ TOTAL**

WINNER:

OFFICIAL SCORES

JUDGE:	JUDGE:	JUDGE:

DATE:

CITY:

VENUE:

REFEREE:

WEIGHT DIVISION:

TITLE:

NOTES:

Boxing judges are trained to score matches using the following criteria:

1. Clean punching (power versus quantity)
2. Effective aggressiveness
3. Ring generalship
4. Defense

Source: Association of Boxing Commissions Regulatory Guidelines

FIGHTNEWS.COM® BOXING SCORECARD

BOXER NAME					BOXER NAME			DATE:
			VS					

RUNNING TOTAL	POINTS DEDUCTED	ROUND SCORE	ROUND	ROUND SCORE	POINTS DEDUCTED	RUNNING TOTAL
			1			
			2			
			3			
			4			
			5			
			6			
			7			
			8			
			9			
			10			
			11			
			12			

DATE:

CITY:

VENUE:

REFEREE:

WEIGHT DIVISION:

TITLE:

NOTES:

TOTAL ⇒   **⇐ TOTAL**

WINNER:

OFFICIAL SCORES

JUDGE:	JUDGE:	JUDGE:

Boxing judges are trained to score matches using the following criteria:

1. Clean punching (power versus quantity)
2. Effective aggressiveness
3. Ring generalship
4. Defense

Source: Association of Boxing Commissions Regulatory Guidelines

FIGHTNEWS.COM® BOXING SCORECARD

| BOXER NAME | | | | | | BOXER NAME | | |

VS

RUNNING TOTAL	POINTS DEDUCTED	ROUND SCORE	ROUND	ROUND SCORE	POINTS DEDUCTED	RUNNING TOTAL
			1			
			2			
			3			
			4			
			5			
			6			
			7			
			8			
			9			
			10			
			11			
			12			

TOTAL ⇒ | | | **⇐ TOTAL**

WINNER:

OFFICIAL SCORES

JUDGE:	JUDGE:	JUDGE:

DATE:
CITY:
VENUE:
REFEREE:
WEIGHT DIVISION:
TITLE:
NOTES:

Boxing judges are trained to score matches using the following criteria:

1. Clean punching (power versus quantity)
2. Effective aggressiveness
3. Ring generalship
4. Defense

Source: Association of Boxing Commissions Regulatory Guidelines

FIGHTNEWS.COM® BOXING SCORECARD

BOXER NAME   BOXER NAME

VS

RUNNING TOTAL	POINTS DEDUCTED	ROUND SCORE	ROUND	ROUND SCORE	POINTS DEDUCTED	RUNNING TOTAL
			1			
			2			
			3			
			4			
			5			
			6			
			7			
			8			
			9			
			10			
			11			
			12			

TOTAL ⇒   **⇐ TOTAL**

WINNER:

OFFICIAL SCORES

JUDGE:	JUDGE:	JUDGE:

DATE:

CITY:

VENUE:

REFEREE:

WEIGHT DIVISION:

TITLE:

NOTES:

Boxing judges are trained to score matches using the following criteria:

1. Clean punching (power versus quantity)
2. Effective aggressiveness
3. Ring generalship
4. Defense

Source: Association of Boxing Commissions Regulatory Guidelines

FIGHTNEWS.COM® BOXING SCORECARD

BOXER NAME   BOXER NAME

VS

RUNNING TOTAL	POINTS DEDUCTED	ROUND SCORE	ROUND	ROUND SCORE	POINTS DEDUCTED	RUNNING TOTAL
			1			
			2			
			3			
			4			
			5			
			6			
			7			
			8			
			9			
			10			
			11			
			12			

TOTAL ⇒ [ ] [ ] **⇐ TOTAL**

WINNER:

OFFICIAL SCORES

JUDGE: JUDGE: JUDGE:

DATE:

CITY:

VENUE:

REFEREE:

WEIGHT DIVISION:

TITLE:

NOTES:

Boxing judges are trained to score matches using the following criteria:

1. Clean punching (power versus quantity)
2. Effective aggressiveness
3. Ring generalship
4. Defense

Source: Association of Boxing Commissions Regulatory Guidelines

FIGHTNEWS.COM® BOXING SCORECARD

BOXER NAME			VS		BOXER NAME			DATE:

RUNNING TOTAL	POINTS DEDUCTED	ROUND SCORE	ROUND	ROUND SCORE	POINTS DEDUCTED	RUNNING TOTAL
			1			
			2			
			3			
			4			
			5			
			6			
			7			
			8			
			9			
			10			
			11			
			12			

TOTAL ⇒ [ ] [ ] **⇐ TOTAL**

DATE:

CITY:

VENUE:

REFEREE:

WEIGHT DIVISION:

TITLE:

NOTES:

WINNER:

OFFICIAL SCORES

JUDGE:	JUDGE:	JUDGE:

Boxing judges are trained to score matches using the following criteria:

1. Clean punching (power versus quantity)
2. Effective aggressiveness
3. Ring generalship
4. Defense

Source: Association of Boxing Commissions Regulatory Guidelines

FIGHTNEWS.COM® BOXING SCORECARD

BOXER NAME							BOXER NAME
			VS				

RUNNING TOTAL	POINTS DEDUCTED	ROUND SCORE	ROUND	ROUND SCORE	POINTS DEDUCTED	RUNNING TOTAL
			1			
			2			
			3			
			4			
			5			
			6			
			7			
			8			
			9			
			10			
			11			
			12			

TOTAL ⇒ [ ] [ ] **⇐ TOTAL**

WINNER:

OFFICIAL SCORES

JUDGE:	JUDGE:	JUDGE:

DATE:

CITY:

VENUE:

REFEREE:

WEIGHT DIVISION:

TITLE:

NOTES:

Boxing judges are trained to score matches using the following criteria:

1. Clean punching (power versus quantity)
2. Effective aggressiveness
3. Ring generalship
4. Defense

Source: Association of Boxing Commissions Regulatory Guidelines

FIGHTNEWS.COM® BOXING SCORECARD

BOXER NAME							BOXER NAME

VS

RUNNING TOTAL	POINTS DEDUCTED	ROUND SCORE	ROUND	ROUND SCORE	POINTS DEDUCTED	RUNNING TOTAL
			1			
			2			
			3			
			4			
			5			
			6			
			7			
			8			
			9			
			10			
			11			
			12			

TOTAL ⇒ | | **⇐ TOTAL**

DATE:
CITY:
VENUE:
REFEREE:
WEIGHT DIVISION:
TITLE:
NOTES:

WINNER:

OFFICIAL SCORES

JUDGE:	JUDGE:	JUDGE:

Boxing judges are trained to score matches using the following criteria:

1. Clean punching (power versus quantity)
2. Effective aggressiveness
3. Ring generalship
4. Defense

Source: Association of Boxing Commissions Regulatory Guidelines

FIGHTNEWS.COM® BOXING SCORECARD

BOXER NAME						BOXER NAME	

VS

RUNNING TOTAL	POINTS DEDUCTED	ROUND SCORE	ROUND	ROUND SCORE	POINTS DEDUCTED	RUNNING TOTAL
			1			
			2			
			3			
			4			
			5			
			6			
			7			
			8			
			9			
			10			
			11			
			12			

TOTAL ⟹ [ ] [ ] **⟸ TOTAL**

WINNER:

OFFICIAL SCORES

JUDGE:	JUDGE:	JUDGE:

DATE:
CITY:
VENUE:
REFEREE:
WEIGHT DIVISION:
TITLE:
NOTES:

Boxing judges are trained to score matches using the following criteria:

1. Clean punching (power versus quantity)
2. Effective aggressiveness
3. Ring generalship
4. Defense

Source: Association of Boxing Commissions Regulatory Guidelines

FIGHTNEWS.COM® BOXING SCORECARD

BOXER NAME						BOXER NAME	

VS

RUNNING TOTAL	POINTS DEDUCTED	ROUND SCORE	ROUND	ROUND SCORE	POINTS DEDUCTED	RUNNING TOTAL
			1			
			2			
			3			
			4			
			5			
			6			
			7			
			8			
			9			
			10			
			11			
			12			

TOTAL ⇒ [   ] [   ] **⇐ TOTAL**

DATE:
CITY:
VENUE:
REFEREE:
WEIGHT DIVISION:
TITLE:
NOTES:

WINNER:

OFFICIAL SCORES

JUDGE:	JUDGE:	JUDGE:

Boxing judges are trained to score matches using the following criteria:

1. Clean punching (power versus quantity)
2. Effective aggressiveness
3. Ring generalship
4. Defense

Source: Association of Boxing Commissions Regulatory Guidelines

FIGHTNEWS.COM® BOXING SCORECARD

BOXER NAME   BOXER NAME

VS

RUNNING TOTAL	POINTS DEDUCTED	ROUND SCORE	ROUND	ROUND SCORE	POINTS DEDUCTED	RUNNING TOTAL
			1			
			2			
			3			
			4			
			5			
			6			
			7			
			8			
			9			
			10			
			11			
			12			

TOTAL ⇒   **⇐ TOTAL**

WINNER:

OFFICIAL SCORES

JUDGE: JUDGE: JUDGE:

DATE:

CITY:

VENUE:

REFEREE:

WEIGHT DIVISION:

TITLE:

NOTES:

Boxing judges are trained to score matches using the following criteria:

1. Clean punching (power versus quantity)
2. Effective aggressiveness
3. Ring generalship
4. Defense

Source: Association of Boxing Commissions Regulatory Guidelines

FIGHTNEWS.COM® BOXING SCORECARD

BOXER NAME   BOXER NAME

VS

RUNNING TOTAL	POINTS DEDUCTED	ROUND SCORE	ROUND	ROUND SCORE	POINTS DEDUCTED	RUNNING TOTAL
			1			
			2			
			3			
			4			
			5			
			6			
			7			
			8			
			9			
			10			
			11			
			12			

TOTAL ⇒   **⇐ TOTAL**

WINNER:

OFFICIAL SCORES

JUDGE:	JUDGE:	JUDGE:

DATE:

CITY:

VENUE:

REFEREE:

WEIGHT DIVISION:

TITLE:

NOTES:

Boxing judges are trained to score matches using the following criteria:

1. Clean punching (power versus quantity)
2. Effective aggressiveness
3. Ring generalship
4. Defense

Source: Association of Boxing Commissions Regulatory Guidelines

FIGHTNEWS.COM® BOXING SCORECARD

BOXER NAME   BOXER NAME

VS

DATE:

CITY:

VENUE:

REFEREE:

WEIGHT DIVISION:

TITLE:

NOTES:

RUNNING TOTAL	POINTS DEDUCTED	ROUND SCORE	ROUND	ROUND SCORE	POINTS DEDUCTED	RUNNING TOTAL
			1			
			2			
			3			
			4			
			5			
			6			
			7			
			8			
			9			
			10			
			11			
			12			

TOTAL ⇒   **⇐ TOTAL**

WINNER:

OFFICIAL SCORES

JUDGE:	JUDGE:	JUDGE:

Boxing judges are trained to score matches using the following criteria:

1. Clean punching (power versus quantity)
2. Effective aggressiveness
3. Ring generalship
4. Defense

Source: Association of Boxing Commissions Regulatory Guidelines

FIGHTNEWS.COM® BOXING SCORECARD

BOXER NAME   BOXER NAME

VS

RUNNING TOTAL	POINTS DEDUCTED	ROUND SCORE	ROUND	ROUND SCORE	POINTS DEDUCTED	RUNNING TOTAL
			1			
			2			
			3			
			4			
			5			
			6			
			7			
			8			
			9			
			10			
			11			
			12			

TOTAL ⇒   **⇐ TOTAL**

WINNER:

OFFICIAL SCORES

JUDGE: JUDGE: JUDGE:

DATE:

CITY:

VENUE:

REFEREE:

WEIGHT DIVISION:

TITLE:

NOTES:

Boxing judges are trained to score matches using the following criteria:

1. Clean punching (power versus quantity)
2. Effective aggressiveness
3. Ring generalship
4. Defense

Source: Association of Boxing Commissions Regulatory Guidelines

FIGHTNEWS.COM® BOXING SCORECARD

BOXER NAME		VS			BOXER NAME		

RUNNING TOTAL	POINTS DEDUCTED	ROUND SCORE	ROUND	ROUND SCORE	POINTS DEDUCTED	RUNNING TOTAL
			1			
			2			
			3			
			4			
			5			
			6			
			7			
			8			
			9			
			10			
			11			
			12			

TOTAL ⇒ | | **⇐ TOTAL**

DATE:

CITY:

VENUE:

REFEREE:

WEIGHT DIVISION:

TITLE:

NOTES:

WINNER:

OFFICIAL SCORES

JUDGE:	JUDGE:	JUDGE:

Boxing judges are trained to score matches using the following criteria:

1. Clean punching (power versus quantity)
2. Effective aggressiveness
3. Ring generalship
4. Defense

Source: Association of Boxing Commissions Regulatory Guidelines

FIGHTNEWS.COM® BOXING SCORECARD

BOXER NAME						BOXER NAME		DATE:

VS

RUNNING TOTAL	POINTS DEDUCTED	ROUND SCORE	ROUND	ROUND SCORE	POINTS DEDUCTED	RUNNING TOTAL
			1			
			2			
			3			
			4			
			5			
			6			
			7			
			8			
			9			
			10			
			11			
			12			

TOTAL ⇒ | | | ⇐ **TOTAL**

DATE:

CITY:

VENUE:

REFEREE:

WEIGHT DIVISION:

TITLE:

NOTES:

WINNER:

OFFICIAL SCORES

JUDGE:	JUDGE:	JUDGE:

Boxing judges are trained to score matches using the following criteria:

1. Clean punching (power versus quantity)
2. Effective aggressiveness
3. Ring generalship
4. Defense

Source: Association of Boxing Commissions Regulatory Guidelines

FIGHTNEWS.COM® BOXING SCORECARD

BOXER NAME | BOXER NAME | DATE:

VS

RUNNING TOTAL	POINTS DEDUCTED	ROUND SCORE	ROUND	ROUND SCORE	POINTS DEDUCTED	RUNNING TOTAL
			1			
			2			
			3			
			4			
			5			
			6			
			7			
			8			
			9			
			10			
			11			
			12			

TOTAL ⇒ [ ] [ ] **⇐ TOTAL**

WINNER:

OFFICIAL SCORES

JUDGE:	JUDGE:	JUDGE:

DATE:

CITY:

VENUE:

REFEREE:

WEIGHT DIVISION:

TITLE:

NOTES:

Boxing judges are trained to score matches using the following criteria:

1. Clean punching (power versus quantity)
2. Effective aggressiveness
3. Ring generalship
4. Defense

Source: Association of Boxing Commissions Regulatory Guidelines

FIGHTNEWS.COM® BOXING SCORECARD

BOXER NAME							
			VS				

RUNNING TOTAL	POINTS DEDUCTED	ROUND SCORE	ROUND	ROUND SCORE	POINTS DEDUCTED	RUNNING TOTAL
			1			
			2			
			3			
			4			
			5			
			6			
			7			
			8			
			9			
			10			
			11			
			12			

TOTAL ⇒ [ ] [ ] **⇐ TOTAL**

WINNER:

OFFICIAL SCORES

JUDGE:	JUDGE:	JUDGE:

DATE:
CITY:
VENUE:
REFEREE:
WEIGHT DIVISION:
TITLE:
NOTES:

Boxing judges are trained to score matches using the following criteria:

1. Clean punching (power versus quantity)
2. Effective aggressiveness
3. Ring generalship
4. Defense

Source: Association of Boxing Commissions Regulatory Guidelines

FIGHTNEWS.COM® BOXING SCORECARD

BOXER NAME   BOXER NAME

VS

RUNNING TOTAL	POINTS DEDUCTED	ROUND SCORE	ROUND	ROUND SCORE	POINTS DEDUCTED	RUNNING TOTAL
			1			
			2			
			3			
			4			
			5			
			6			
			7			
			8			
			9			
			10			
			11			
			12			

TOTAL ⇒ [ ] [ ] **⇐ TOTAL**

WINNER:

OFFICIAL SCORES

JUDGE:	JUDGE:	JUDGE:

DATE:

CITY:

VENUE:

REFEREE:

WEIGHT DIVISION:

TITLE:

NOTES:

Boxing judges are trained to score matches using the following criteria:

1. Clean punching (power versus quantity)
2. Effective aggressiveness
3. Ring generalship
4. Defense

Source: Association of Boxing Commissions Regulatory Guidelines

FIGHTNEWS.COM® BOXING SCORECARD

BOXER NAME					BOXER NAME			DATE:
		VS						
								CITY:

RUNNING TOTAL	POINTS DEDUCTED	ROUND SCORE	ROUND	ROUND SCORE	POINTS DEDUCTED	RUNNING TOTAL
			1			
			2			
			3			
			4			
			5			
			6			
			7			
			8			
			9			
			10			
			11			
			12			

TOTAL ⇒ [ ] [ ] ⇐ **TOTAL**

VENUE:

REFEREE:

WEIGHT DIVISION:

TITLE:

NOTES:

WINNER:

OFFICIAL SCORES

JUDGE:	JUDGE:	JUDGE:

Boxing judges are trained to score matches using the following criteria:

1. Clean punching (power versus quantity)
2. Effective aggressiveness
3. Ring generalship
4. Defense

Source: Association of Boxing Commissions Regulatory Guidelines

FIGHTNEWS.COM® BOXING SCORECARD

BOXER NAME   BOXER NAME

VS

RUNNING TOTAL	POINTS DEDUCTED	ROUND SCORE	ROUND	ROUND SCORE	POINTS DEDUCTED	RUNNING TOTAL
			1			
			2			
			3			
			4			
			5			
			6			
			7			
			8			
			9			
			10			
			11			
			12			

TOTAL ⟹ [ ] [ ] **⟸ TOTAL**

WINNER:

OFFICIAL SCORES

JUDGE:	JUDGE:	JUDGE:

DATE:

CITY:

VENUE:

REFEREE:

WEIGHT DIVISION:

TITLE:

NOTES:

Boxing judges are trained to score matches using the following criteria:

1. Clean punching (power versus quantity)
2. Effective aggressiveness
3. Ring generalship
4. Defense

Source: Association of Boxing Commissions Regulatory Guidelines

FIGHTNEWS.COM® BOXING SCORECARD

BOXER NAME				BOXER NAME			DATE:
		VS					CITY:

RUNNING TOTAL	POINTS DEDUCTED	ROUND SCORE	ROUND	ROUND SCORE	POINTS DEDUCTED	RUNNING TOTAL
			1			
			2			
			3			
			4			
			5			
			6			
			7			
			8			
			9			
			10			
			11			
			12			

VENUE:

REFEREE:

WEIGHT DIVISION:

TITLE:

NOTES:

TOTAL ⇒ ☐ ☐ **⇐ TOTAL**

WINNER:

OFFICIAL SCORES

JUDGE:	JUDGE:	JUDGE:

Boxing judges are trained to score matches using the following criteria:

1. Clean punching (power versus quantity)
2. Effective aggressiveness
3. Ring generalship
4. Defense

Source: Association of Boxing Commissions Regulatory Guidelines

FIGHTNEWS.COM® BOXING SCORECARD

BOXER NAME			VS		BOXER NAME	

RUNNING TOTAL	POINTS DEDUCTED	ROUND SCORE	ROUND	ROUND SCORE	POINTS DEDUCTED	RUNNING TOTAL
			1			
			2			
			3			
			4			
			5			
			6			
			7			
			8			
			9			
			10			
			11			
			12			
TOTAL ⇒					**⇐ TOTAL**	

DATE:
CITY:
VENUE:
REFEREE:
WEIGHT DIVISION:
TITLE:
NOTES:

WINNER:

OFFICIAL SCORES

JUDGE:	JUDGE:	JUDGE:

Boxing judges are trained to score matches using the following criteria:

1. Clean punching (power versus quantity)
2. Effective aggressiveness
3. Ring generalship
4. Defense

Source: Association of Boxing Commissions Regulatory Guidelines

FIGHTNEWS.COM® BOXING SCORECARD

BOXER NAME			VS		BOXER NAME	

DATE:
CITY:
VENUE:
REFEREE:
WEIGHT DIVISION:
TITLE:
NOTES:

RUNNING TOTAL	POINTS DEDUCTED	ROUND SCORE	ROUND	ROUND SCORE	POINTS DEDUCTED	RUNNING TOTAL
			1			
			2			
			3			
			4			
			5			
			6			
			7			
			8			
			9			
			10			
			11			
			12			

TOTAL ⇒ [ ] [ ] **⇐ TOTAL**

WINNER:

OFFICIAL SCORES

JUDGE:	JUDGE:	JUDGE:

Boxing judges are trained to score matches using the following criteria:

1. Clean punching (power versus quantity)
2. Effective aggressiveness
3. Ring generalship
4. Defense

Source: Association of Boxing Commissions Regulatory Guidelines

FIGHTNEWS.COM® BOXING SCORECARD

BOXER NAME			VS			BOXER NAME		DATE:

RUNNING TOTAL	POINTS DEDUCTED	ROUND SCORE	ROUND	ROUND SCORE	POINTS DEDUCTED	RUNNING TOTAL
			1			
			2			
			3			
			4			
			5			
			6			
			7			
			8			
			9			
			10			
			11			
			12			
TOTAL ⇒						**⇐ TOTAL**

DATE:

CITY:

VENUE:

REFEREE:

WEIGHT DIVISION:

TITLE:

NOTES:

WINNER:

OFFICIAL SCORES

JUDGE:	JUDGE:	JUDGE:

Boxing judges are trained to score matches using the following criteria:

1. Clean punching (power versus quantity)
2. Effective aggressiveness
3. Ring generalship
4. Defense

Source: Association of Boxing Commissions Regulatory Guidelines

FIGHTNEWS.COM® BOXING SCORECARD

BOXER NAME						BOXER NAME		DATE:
			VS					

RUNNING TOTAL	POINTS DEDUCTED	ROUND SCORE	ROUND	ROUND SCORE	POINTS DEDUCTED	RUNNING TOTAL
			1			
			2			
			3			
			4			
			5			
			6			
			7			
			8			
			9			
			10			
			11			
			12			

DATE:

CITY:

VENUE:

REFEREE:

WEIGHT DIVISION:

TITLE:

NOTES:

TOTAL ⇒ [   ] [   ] **⇐ TOTAL**

WINNER:

OFFICIAL SCORES

JUDGE:	JUDGE:	JUDGE:

Boxing judges are trained to score matches using the following criteria:

1. Clean punching (power versus quantity)
2. Effective aggressiveness
3. Ring generalship
4. Defense

Source: Association of Boxing Commissions Regulatory Guidelines

FIGHTNEWS.COM® BOXING SCORECARD

BOXER NAME			VS		BOXER NAME			DATE:

RUNNING TOTAL	POINTS DEDUCTED	ROUND SCORE	ROUND	ROUND SCORE	POINTS DEDUCTED	RUNNING TOTAL
			1			
			2			
			3			
			4			
			5			
			6			
			7			
			8			
			9			
			10			
			11			
			12			
TOTAL ⇒					**⇐ TOTAL**	

DATE:

CITY:

VENUE:

REFEREE:

WEIGHT DIVISION:

TITLE:

NOTES:

WINNER:

OFFICIAL SCORES

JUDGE:	JUDGE:	JUDGE:

Boxing judges are trained to score matches using the following criteria:

1. Clean punching (power versus quantity)
2. Effective aggressiveness
3. Ring generalship
4. Defense

Source: Association of Boxing Commissions Regulatory Guidelines

FIGHTNEWS.COM® BOXING SCORECARD

BOXER NAME   BOXER NAME

VS

RUNNING TOTAL	POINTS DEDUCTED	ROUND SCORE	ROUND	ROUND SCORE	POINTS DEDUCTED	RUNNING TOTAL
			1			
			2			
			3			
			4			
			5			
			6			
			7			
			8			
			9			
			10			
			11			
			12			

TOTAL ⇒ [　　] [　　] **⇐ TOTAL**

WINNER:

OFFICIAL SCORES

JUDGE:	JUDGE:	JUDGE:

DATE:

CITY:

VENUE:

REFEREE:

WEIGHT DIVISION:

TITLE:

NOTES:

Boxing judges are trained to score matches using the following criteria:

1. Clean punching (power versus quantity)
2. Effective aggressiveness
3. Ring generalship
4. Defense

Source: Association of Boxing Commissions Regulatory Guidelines

FIGHTNEWS.COM® BOXING SCORECARD

BOXER NAME   BOXER NAME

VS

RUNNING TOTAL	POINTS DEDUCTED	ROUND SCORE	ROUND	ROUND SCORE	POINTS DEDUCTED	RUNNING TOTAL
			1			
			2			
			3			
			4			
			5			
			6			
			7			
			8			
			9			
			10			
			11			
			12			

TOTAL ⇒ [   ] [   ] **⇐ TOTAL**

WINNER:

OFFICIAL SCORES

JUDGE:	JUDGE:	JUDGE:

DATE:

CITY:

VENUE:

REFEREE:

WEIGHT DIVISION:

TITLE:

NOTES:

Boxing judges are trained to score matches using the following criteria:

1. Clean punching (power versus quantity)
2. Effective aggressiveness
3. Ring generalship
4. Defense

Source: Association of Boxing Commissions Regulatory Guidelines

FIGHTNEWS.COM® BOXING SCORECARD

BOXER NAME   BOXER NAME

VS

RUNNING TOTAL	POINTS DEDUCTED	ROUND SCORE	ROUND	ROUND SCORE	POINTS DEDUCTED	RUNNING TOTAL
			1			
			2			
			3			
			4			
			5			
			6			
			7			
			8			
			9			
			10			
			11			
			12			

TOTAL ⇒ [   ] [   ] **⇐ TOTAL**

WINNER:

OFFICIAL SCORES

JUDGE:	JUDGE:	JUDGE:

DATE:

CITY:

VENUE:

REFEREE:

WEIGHT DIVISION:

TITLE:

NOTES:

Boxing judges are trained to score matches using the following criteria:

1. Clean punching (power versus quantity)
2. Effective aggressiveness
3. Ring generalship
4. Defense

Source: Association of Boxing Commissions Regulatory Guidelines

FIGHTNEWS.COM® BOXING SCORECARD

BOXER NAME   BOXER NAME

VS

RUNNING TOTAL	POINTS DEDUCTED	ROUND SCORE	ROUND	ROUND SCORE	POINTS DEDUCTED	RUNNING TOTAL
			1			
			2			
			3			
			4			
			5			
			6			
			7			
			8			
			9			
			10			
			11			
			12			

TOTAL ⇒ [ ] [ ] **⇐ TOTAL**

WINNER:

OFFICIAL SCORES

JUDGE:	JUDGE:	JUDGE:

DATE:

CITY:

VENUE:

REFEREE:

WEIGHT DIVISION:

TITLE:

NOTES:

Boxing judges are trained to score matches using the following criteria:

1. Clean punching (power versus quantity)
2. Effective aggressiveness
3. Ring generalship
4. Defense

Source: Association of Boxing Commissions Regulatory Guidelines

FIGHTNEWS.COM® BOXING SCORECARD

BOXER NAME   BOXER NAME   DATE:

VS

CITY:

RUNNING TOTAL	POINTS DEDUCTED	ROUND SCORE	ROUND	ROUND SCORE	POINTS DEDUCTED	RUNNING TOTAL
			1			
			2			
			3			
			4			
			5			
			6			
			7			
			8			
			9			
			10			
			11			
			12			

VENUE:

REFEREE:

WEIGHT DIVISION:

TITLE:

NOTES:

TOTAL ⟹ [ ] [ ] **⟸ TOTAL**

WINNER:

OFFICIAL SCORES

JUDGE:	JUDGE:	JUDGE:

Boxing judges are trained to score matches using the following criteria:

1. Clean punching (power versus quantity)
2. Effective aggressiveness
3. Ring generalship
4. Defense

Source: Association of Boxing Commissions Regulatory Guidelines

FIGHTNEWS.COM® BOXING SCORECARD

BOXER NAME			VS			BOXER NAME		DATE:

RUNNING TOTAL	POINTS DEDUCTED	ROUND SCORE	ROUND	ROUND SCORE	POINTS DEDUCTED	RUNNING TOTAL
			1			
			2			
			3			
			4			
			5			
			6			
			7			
			8			
			9			
			10			
			11			
			12			
TOTAL ⇒					**⇐ TOTAL**	

CITY:

VENUE:

REFEREE:

WEIGHT DIVISION:

TITLE:

NOTES:

WINNER:

OFFICIAL SCORES

JUDGE:	JUDGE:	JUDGE:

Boxing judges are trained to score matches using the following criteria:

1. Clean punching (power versus quantity)
2. Effective aggressiveness
3. Ring generalship
4. Defense

Source: Association of Boxing Commissions Regulatory Guidelines

FIGHTNEWS.COM® BOXING SCORECARD

BOXER NAME			VS		BOXER NAME			DATE:

RUNNING TOTAL	POINTS DEDUCTED	ROUND SCORE	ROUND	ROUND SCORE	POINTS DEDUCTED	RUNNING TOTAL
			1			
			2			
			3			
			4			
			5			
			6			
			7			
			8			
			9			
			10			
			11			
			12			

TOTAL ⇒ [ ] [ ] **⇐ TOTAL**

WINNER:

OFFICIAL SCORES

JUDGE:	JUDGE:	JUDGE:

DATE:

CITY:

VENUE:

REFEREE:

WEIGHT DIVISION:

TITLE:

NOTES:

Boxing judges are trained to score matches using the following criteria:

1. Clean punching (power versus quantity)
2. Effective aggressiveness
3. Ring generalship
4. Defense

Source: Association of Boxing Commissions Regulatory Guidelines

FIGHTNEWS.COM® BOXING SCORECARD

BOXER NAME			VS			BOXER NAME

RUNNING TOTAL	POINTS DEDUCTED	ROUND SCORE	ROUND	ROUND SCORE	POINTS DEDUCTED	RUNNING TOTAL
			1			
			2			
			3			
			4			
			5			
			6			
			7			
			8			
			9			
			10			
			11			
			12			
TOTAL ⇒					**⇐ TOTAL**	

WINNER:

OFFICIAL SCORES

JUDGE:	JUDGE:	JUDGE:

DATE:

CITY:

VENUE:

REFEREE:

WEIGHT DIVISION:

TITLE:

NOTES:

Boxing judges are trained to score matches using the following criteria:

1. Clean punching (power versus quantity)
2. Effective aggressiveness
3. Ring generalship
4. Defense

Source: Association of Boxing Commissions Regulatory Guidelines

FIGHTNEWS.COM® BOXING SCORECARD

BOXER NAME				BOXER NAME			DATE:
			VS				CITY:

RUNNING TOTAL	POINTS DEDUCTED	ROUND SCORE	ROUND	ROUND SCORE	POINTS DEDUCTED	RUNNING TOTAL
			1			
			2			
			3			
			4			
			5			
			6			
			7			
			8			
			9			
			10			
			11			
			12			

TOTAL ⇒ | | **⇐ TOTAL**

VENUE:

REFEREE:

WEIGHT DIVISION:

TITLE:

NOTES:

WINNER:

OFFICIAL SCORES

JUDGE:	JUDGE:	JUDGE:

Boxing judges are trained to score matches using the following criteria:

1. Clean punching (power versus quantity)
2. Effective aggressiveness
3. Ring generalship
4. Defense

Source: Association of Boxing Commissions Regulatory Guidelines

FIGHTNEWS.COM® BOXING SCORECARD

BOXER NAME			VS			BOXER NAME

RUNNING TOTAL	POINTS DEDUCTED	ROUND SCORE	ROUND	ROUND SCORE	POINTS DEDUCTED	RUNNING TOTAL
			1			
			2			
			3			
			4			
			5			
			6			
			7			
			8			
			9			
			10			
			11			
			12			

TOTAL ⇒ [   ] [   ] **⇐ TOTAL**

WINNER:

OFFICIAL SCORES

JUDGE:	JUDGE:	JUDGE:

DATE:

CITY:

VENUE:

REFEREE:

WEIGHT DIVISION:

TITLE:

NOTES:

Boxing judges are trained to score matches using the following criteria:

1. Clean punching (power versus quantity)
2. Effective aggressiveness
3. Ring generalship
4. Defense

Source: Association of Boxing Commissions Regulatory Guidelines

FIGHTNEWS.COM® BOXING SCORECARD

BOXER NAME					BOXER NAME			DATE:
			VS					

RUNNING TOTAL	POINTS DEDUCTED	ROUND SCORE	ROUND	ROUND SCORE	POINTS DEDUCTED	RUNNING TOTAL
			1			
			2			
			3			
			4			
			5			
			6			
			7			
			8			
			9			
			10			
			11			
			12			

TOTAL ⇒ ⬜ ⬜ **⇐ TOTAL**

CITY:

VENUE:

REFEREE:

WEIGHT DIVISION:

TITLE:

NOTES:

WINNER:

OFFICIAL SCORES

JUDGE:	JUDGE:	JUDGE:

Boxing judges are trained to score matches using the following criteria:

1. Clean punching (power versus quantity)
2. Effective aggressiveness
3. Ring generalship
4. Defense

Source: Association of Boxing Commissions Regulatory Guidelines

FIGHTNEWS.COM® BOXING SCORECARD

BOXER NAME			VS		BOXER NAME	

RUNNING TOTAL	POINTS DEDUCTED	ROUND SCORE	ROUND	ROUND SCORE	POINTS DEDUCTED	RUNNING TOTAL
			1			
			2			
			3			
			4			
			5			
			6			
			7			
			8			
			9			
			10			
			11			
			12			

TOTAL ⇒ [   ] [   ] **⇐ TOTAL**

WINNER:

OFFICIAL SCORES

JUDGE:	JUDGE:	JUDGE:

DATE:

CITY:

VENUE:

REFEREE:

WEIGHT DIVISION:

TITLE:

NOTES:

Boxing judges are trained to score matches using the following criteria:

1. Clean punching (power versus quantity)
2. Effective aggressiveness
3. Ring generalship
4. Defense

Source: Association of Boxing Commissions Regulatory Guidelines

FIGHTNEWS.COM® BOXING SCORECARD

BOXER NAME   BOXER NAME

VS

RUNNING TOTAL	POINTS DEDUCTED	ROUND SCORE	ROUND	ROUND SCORE	POINTS DEDUCTED	RUNNING TOTAL
			1			
			2			
			3			
			4			
			5			
			6			
			7			
			8			
			9			
			10			
			11			
			12			

TOTAL ⇒ [ ] [ ] **⇐ TOTAL**

WINNER:

OFFICIAL SCORES

JUDGE:	JUDGE:	JUDGE:

DATE:

CITY:

VENUE:

REFEREE:

WEIGHT DIVISION:

TITLE:

NOTES:

Boxing judges are trained to score matches using the following criteria:

1. Clean punching (power versus quantity)
2. Effective aggressiveness
3. Ring generalship
4. Defense

Source: Association of Boxing Commissions Regulatory Guidelines

FIGHTNEWS.COM® BOXING SCORECARD

BOXER NAME					BOXER NAME			DATE:
		VS						CITY:

RUNNING TOTAL	POINTS DEDUCTED	ROUND SCORE	ROUND	ROUND SCORE	POINTS DEDUCTED	RUNNING TOTAL
			1			
			2			
			3			
			4			
			5			
			6			
			7			
			8			
			9			
			10			
			11			
			12			

TOTAL ⇒ [ ] [ ] **⇐ TOTAL**

DATE:

CITY:

VENUE:

REFEREE:

WEIGHT DIVISION:

TITLE:

NOTES:

WINNER:

OFFICIAL SCORES

JUDGE:	JUDGE:	JUDGE:

Boxing judges are trained to score matches using the following criteria:

1. Clean punching (power versus quantity)
2. Effective aggressiveness
3. Ring generalship
4. Defense

Source: Association of Boxing Commissions Regulatory Guidelines

FIGHTNEWS.COM® BOXING SCORECARD

BOXER NAME				VS		BOXER NAME		

RUNNING TOTAL	POINTS DEDUCTED	ROUND SCORE	ROUND	ROUND SCORE	POINTS DEDUCTED	RUNNING TOTAL
			1			
			2			
			3			
			4			
			5			
			6			
			7			
			8			
			9			
			10			
			11			
			12			

TOTAL ⇒ ☐ ☐ **⇐ TOTAL**

WINNER:

OFFICIAL SCORES

JUDGE:	JUDGE:	JUDGE:

DATE:

CITY:

VENUE:

REFEREE:

WEIGHT DIVISION:

TITLE:

NOTES:

Boxing judges are trained to score matches using the following criteria:

1. Clean punching (power versus quantity)
2. Effective aggressiveness
3. Ring generalship
4. Defense

Source: Association of Boxing Commissions Regulatory Guidelines

FIGHTNEWS.COM® BOXING SCORECARD

BOXER NAME   BOXER NAME

VS

RUNNING TOTAL	POINTS DEDUCTED	ROUND SCORE	ROUND	ROUND SCORE	POINTS DEDUCTED	RUNNING TOTAL
			1			
			2			
			3			
			4			
			5			
			6			
			7			
			8			
			9			
			10			
			11			
			12			

TOTAL ⇒ [   ] [   ] **⇐ TOTAL**

WINNER:

OFFICIAL SCORES

JUDGE:	JUDGE:	JUDGE:

DATE:

CITY:

VENUE:

REFEREE:

WEIGHT DIVISION:

TITLE:

NOTES:

Boxing judges are trained to score matches using the following criteria:

1. Clean punching (power versus quantity)
2. Effective aggressiveness
3. Ring generalship
4. Defense

Source: Association of Boxing Commissions Regulatory Guidelines

FIGHTNEWS.COM® BOXING SCORECARD

BOXER NAME			VS		BOXER NAME			DATE:

RUNNING TOTAL	POINTS DEDUCTED	ROUND SCORE	ROUND	ROUND SCORE	POINTS DEDUCTED	RUNNING TOTAL
			1			
			2			
			3			
			4			
			5			
			6			
			7			
			8			
			9			
			10			
			11			
			12			

TOTAL ⇒ | | **⇐ TOTAL**

DATE:

CITY:

VENUE:

REFEREE:

WEIGHT DIVISION:

TITLE:

NOTES:

WINNER:

OFFICIAL SCORES

JUDGE:	JUDGE:	JUDGE:

Boxing judges are trained to score matches using the following criteria:

1. Clean punching (power versus quantity)
2. Effective aggressiveness
3. Ring generalship
4. Defense

Source: Association of Boxing Commissions Regulatory Guidelines

FIGHTNEWS.COM® BOXING SCORECARD

BOXER NAME   BOXER NAME   DATE:

VS   CITY:

RUNNING TOTAL	POINTS DEDUCTED	ROUND SCORE	ROUND	ROUND SCORE	POINTS DEDUCTED	RUNNING TOTAL
			1			
			2			
			3			
			4			
			5			
			6			
			7			
			8			
			9			
			10			
			11			
			12			

VENUE:

REFEREE:

WEIGHT DIVISION:

TITLE:

NOTES:

TOTAL ⇒ [ ] [ ] ⇐ **TOTAL**

WINNER:

OFFICIAL SCORES

JUDGE:	JUDGE:	JUDGE:

Boxing judges are trained to score matches using the following criteria:

1. Clean punching (power versus quantity)
2. Effective aggressiveness
3. Ring generalship
4. Defense

Source: Association of Boxing Commissions Regulatory Guidelines

FIGHTNEWS.COM® BOXING SCORECARD

BOXER NAME			VS		BOXER NAME			DATE:

RUNNING TOTAL	POINTS DEDUCTED	ROUND SCORE	ROUND	ROUND SCORE	POINTS DEDUCTED	RUNNING TOTAL
			1			
			2			
			3			
			4			
			5			
			6			
			7			
			8			
			9			
			10			
			11			
			12			

TOTAL ⇒ [   ] [   ] **⇐ TOTAL**

Side panel:
DATE:
CITY:
VENUE:
REFEREE:
WEIGHT DIVISION:
TITLE:
NOTES:

WINNER:

OFFICIAL SCORES

JUDGE:	JUDGE:	JUDGE:

Boxing judges are trained to score matches using the following criteria:

1. Clean punching (power versus quantity)
2. Effective aggressiveness
3. Ring generalship
4. Defense

Source: Association of Boxing Commissions Regulatory Guidelines

FIGHTNEWS.COM® BOXING SCORECARD

BOXER NAME   VS   BOXER NAME

RUNNING TOTAL	POINTS DEDUCTED	ROUND SCORE	ROUND	ROUND SCORE	POINTS DEDUCTED	RUNNING TOTAL
			1			
			2			
			3			
			4			
			5			
			6			
			7			
			8			
			9			
			10			
			11			
			12			

TOTAL ⇒ [ ] [ ] **⇐ TOTAL**

WINNER:

OFFICIAL SCORES

JUDGE:	JUDGE:	JUDGE:

DATE:

CITY:

VENUE:

REFEREE:

WEIGHT DIVISION:

TITLE:

NOTES:

Boxing judges are trained to score matches using the following criteria:

1. Clean punching (power versus quantity)
2. Effective aggressiveness
3. Ring generalship
4. Defense

Source: Association of Boxing Commissions Regulatory Guidelines

FIGHTNEWS.COM® BOXING SCORECARD

BOXER NAME	BOXER NAME
	VS

RUNNING TOTAL	POINTS DEDUCTED	ROUND SCORE	ROUND	ROUND SCORE	POINTS DEDUCTED	RUNNING TOTAL
			1			
			2			
			3			
			4			
			5			
			6			
			7			
			8			
			9			
			10			
			11			
			12			

TOTAL ⇒ _____ _____ **⇐ TOTAL**

WINNER: _____

OFFICIAL SCORES

JUDGE:	JUDGE:	JUDGE:

DATE:

CITY:

VENUE:

REFEREE:

WEIGHT DIVISION:

TITLE:

NOTES:

Boxing judges are trained to score matches using the following criteria:

1. Clean punching (power versus quantity)
2. Effective aggressiveness
3. Ring generalship
4. Defense

Source: Association of Boxing Commissions Regulatory Guidelines

FIGHTNEWS.COM® BOXING SCORECARD

| BOXER NAME | | | VS | | | BOXER NAME | DATE: |

RUNNING TOTAL	POINTS DEDUCTED	ROUND SCORE	ROUND	ROUND SCORE	POINTS DEDUCTED	RUNNING TOTAL
			1			
			2			
			3			
			4			
			5			
			6			
			7			
			8			
			9			
			10			
			11			
			12			

TOTAL ⇒ [ ] [ ] **⇐ TOTAL**

DATE:

CITY:

VENUE:

REFEREE:

WEIGHT DIVISION:

TITLE:

NOTES:

WINNER:

OFFICIAL SCORES

JUDGE:	JUDGE:	JUDGE:

Boxing judges are trained to score matches using the following criteria:

1. Clean punching (power versus quantity)
2. Effective aggressiveness
3. Ring generalship
4. Defense

Source: Association of Boxing Commissions Regulatory Guidelines

FIGHTNEWS.COM® BOXING SCORECARD

BOXER NAME   **VS**   BOXER NAME

RUNNING TOTAL	POINTS DEDUCTED	ROUND SCORE	ROUND	ROUND SCORE	POINTS DEDUCTED	RUNNING TOTAL
			1			
			2			
			3			
			4			
			5			
			6			
			7			
			8			
			9			
			10			
			11			
			12			

TOTAL ⇒ [ ] [ ] **⇐ TOTAL**

WINNER:

OFFICIAL SCORES

JUDGE:	JUDGE:	JUDGE:

DATE:

CITY:

VENUE:

REFEREE:

WEIGHT DIVISION:

TITLE:

NOTES:

Boxing judges are trained to score matches using the following criteria:

1. Clean punching (power versus quantity)
2. Effective aggressiveness
3. Ring generalship
4. Defense

Source: Association of Boxing Commissions Regulatory Guidelines

FIGHTNEWS.COM® BOXING SCORECARD

BOXER NAME			VS			BOXER NAME		DATE:

RUNNING TOTAL	POINTS DEDUCTED	ROUND SCORE	ROUND	ROUND SCORE	POINTS DEDUCTED	RUNNING TOTAL
			1			
			2			
			3			
			4			
			5			
			6			
			7			
			8			
			9			
			10			
			11			
			12			
TOTAL ⇒					**⇐ TOTAL**	

DATE:

CITY:

VENUE:

REFEREE:

WEIGHT DIVISION:

TITLE:

NOTES:

WINNER:

OFFICIAL SCORES

JUDGE:	JUDGE:	JUDGE:

Boxing judges are trained to score matches using the following criteria:

1. Clean punching (power versus quantity)
2. Effective aggressiveness
3. Ring generalship
4. Defense

Source: Association of Boxing Commissions Regulatory Guidelines

FIGHTNEWS.COM® BOXING SCORECARD

BOXER NAME			VS		BOXER NAME	

RUNNING TOTAL	POINTS DEDUCTED	ROUND SCORE	ROUND	ROUND SCORE	POINTS DEDUCTED	RUNNING TOTAL
			1			
			2			
			3			
			4			
			5			
			6			
			7			
			8			
			9			
			10			
			11			
			12			

TOTAL ⇒ [ ] [ ] **⇐ TOTAL**

WINNER:

OFFICIAL SCORES

JUDGE:	JUDGE:	JUDGE:

DATE:

CITY:

VENUE:

REFEREE:

WEIGHT DIVISION:

TITLE:

NOTES:

Boxing judges are trained to score matches using the following criteria:

1. Clean punching (power versus quantity)
2. Effective aggressiveness
3. Ring generalship
4. Defense

Source: Association of Boxing Commissions Regulatory Guidelines

FIGHTNEWS.COM® BOXING SCORECARD

BOXER NAME   BOXER NAME

VS

RUNNING TOTAL	POINTS DEDUCTED	ROUND SCORE	ROUND	ROUND SCORE	POINTS DEDUCTED	RUNNING TOTAL
			1			
			2			
			3			
			4			
			5			
			6			
			7			
			8			
			9			
			10			
			11			
			12			

TOTAL ⇒ [ ] [ ] **⇐ TOTAL**

WINNER:

OFFICIAL SCORES

JUDGE:	JUDGE:	JUDGE:

DATE:

CITY:

VENUE:

REFEREE:

WEIGHT DIVISION:

TITLE:

NOTES:

Boxing judges are trained to score matches using the following criteria:

1. Clean punching (power versus quantity)
2. Effective aggressiveness
3. Ring generalship
4. Defense

Source: Association of Boxing Commissions Regulatory Guidelines

FIGHTNEWS.COM® BOXING SCORECARD

BOXER NAME							

VS

DATE:

CITY:

RUNNING TOTAL	POINTS DEDUCTED	ROUND SCORE	ROUND	ROUND SCORE	POINTS DEDUCTED	RUNNING TOTAL
			1			
			2			
			3			
			4			
			5			
			6			
			7			
			8			
			9			
			10			
			11			
			12			

TOTAL ⇒ [　] [　] **⇐ TOTAL**

VENUE:

REFEREE:

WEIGHT DIVISION:

TITLE:

NOTES:

WINNER:

OFFICIAL SCORES

JUDGE:	JUDGE:	JUDGE:

Boxing judges are trained to score matches using the following criteria:

1. Clean punching (power versus quantity)
2. Effective aggressiveness
3. Ring generalship
4. Defense

Source: Association of Boxing Commissions Regulatory Guidelines

FIGHTNEWS.COM® BOXING SCORECARD

BOXER NAME				VS			BOXER NAME		DATE:

RUNNING TOTAL	POINTS DEDUCTED	ROUND SCORE	ROUND	ROUND SCORE	POINTS DEDUCTED	RUNNING TOTAL
			1			
			2			
			3			
			4			
			5			
			6			
			7			
			8			
			9			
			10			
			11			
			12			

TOTAL ⟹ [ ] [ ] **⟸ TOTAL**

DATE:

CITY:

VENUE:

REFEREE:

WEIGHT DIVISION:

TITLE:

NOTES:

WINNER:

OFFICIAL SCORES

JUDGE:	JUDGE:	JUDGE:

Boxing judges are trained to score matches using the following criteria:

1. Clean punching (power versus quantity)
2. Effective aggressiveness
3. Ring generalship
4. Defense

Source: Association of Boxing Commissions Regulatory Guidelines

FIGHTNEWS.COM® BOXING SCORECARD

BOXER NAME   BOXER NAME

VS

RUNNING TOTAL	POINTS DEDUCTED	ROUND SCORE	ROUND	ROUND SCORE	POINTS DEDUCTED	RUNNING TOTAL
			1			
			2			
			3			
			4			
			5			
			6			
			7			
			8			
			9			
			10			
			11			
			12			

TOTAL ⇒ [ ] [ ] **⇐ TOTAL**

WINNER:

OFFICIAL SCORES

JUDGE:	JUDGE:	JUDGE:

DATE:

CITY:

VENUE:

REFEREE:

WEIGHT DIVISION:

TITLE:

NOTES:

Boxing judges are trained to score matches using the following criteria:

1. Clean punching (power versus quantity)
2. Effective aggressiveness
3. Ring generalship
4. Defense

Source: Association of Boxing Commissions Regulatory Guidelines

FIGHTNEWS.COM® BOXING SCORECARD

BOXER NAME   BOXER NAME

<u>VS</u>

RUNNING TOTAL	POINTS DEDUCTED	ROUND SCORE	ROUND	ROUND SCORE	POINTS DEDUCTED	RUNNING TOTAL
			1			
			2			
			3			
			4			
			5			
			6			
			7			
			8			
			9			
			10			
			11			
			12			

TOTAL ⇒ [ ] [ ] **⇐ TOTAL**

DATE:
CITY:
VENUE:
REFEREE:
WEIGHT DIVISION:
TITLE:
NOTES:

WINNER:

OFFICIAL SCORES

JUDGE:	JUDGE:	JUDGE:

Boxing judges are trained to score matches using the following criteria:

1. Clean punching (power versus quantity)
2. Effective aggressiveness
3. Ring generalship
4. Defense

Source: Association of Boxing Commissions Regulatory Guidelines

FIGHTNEWS.COM® BOXING SCORECARD

BOXER NAME			VS		BOXER NAME		
RUNNING TOTAL	POINTS DEDUCTED	ROUND SCORE	ROUND	ROUND SCORE	POINTS DEDUCTED	RUNNING TOTAL
			1			
			2			
			3			
			4			
			5			
			6			
			7			
			8			
			9			
			10			
			11			
			12			

TOTAL ⇒ [____] [____] **⇐ TOTAL**

WINNER: [_____]

OFFICIAL SCORES

JUDGE:	JUDGE:	JUDGE:

DATE:

CITY:

VENUE:

REFEREE:

WEIGHT DIVISION:

TITLE:

NOTES:

Boxing judges are trained to score matches using the following criteria:

1. Clean punching (power versus quantity)
2. Effective aggressiveness
3. Ring generalship
4. Defense

Source: Association of Boxing Commissions Regulatory Guidelines

FIGHTNEWS.COM® BOXING SCORECARD

BOXER NAME			VS		BOXER NAME			DATE:

RUNNING TOTAL	POINTS DEDUCTED	ROUND SCORE	ROUND	ROUND SCORE	POINTS DEDUCTED	RUNNING TOTAL
			1			
			2			
			3			
			4			
			5			
			6			
			7			
			8			
			9			
			10			
			11			
			12			
TOTAL ⇒					**⇐ TOTAL**	

CITY:

VENUE:

REFEREE:

WEIGHT DIVISION:

TITLE:

NOTES:

WINNER:

OFFICIAL SCORES

JUDGE:	JUDGE:	JUDGE:

Boxing judges are trained to score matches using the following criteria:

1. Clean punching (power versus quantity)
2. Effective aggressiveness
3. Ring generalship
4. Defense

Source: Association of Boxing Commissions Regulatory Guidelines

FIGHTNEWS.COM® BOXING SCORECARD

BOXER NAME				BOXER NAME			DATE:
			VS				

RUNNING TOTAL	POINTS DEDUCTED	ROUND SCORE	ROUND	ROUND SCORE	POINTS DEDUCTED	RUNNING TOTAL
			1			
			2			
			3			
			4			
			5			
			6			
			7			
			8			
			9			
			10			
			11			
			12			

TOTAL ⇒ [ ] [ ] **⇐ TOTAL**

DATE:

CITY:

VENUE:

REFEREE:

WEIGHT DIVISION:

TITLE:

NOTES:

WINNER:

OFFICIAL SCORES

JUDGE:	JUDGE:	JUDGE:

Boxing judges are trained to score matches using the following criteria:

1. Clean punching (power versus quantity)
2. Effective aggressiveness
3. Ring generalship
4. Defense

Source: Association of Boxing Commissions Regulatory Guidelines

FIGHTNEWS.COM® BOXING SCORECARD

BOXER NAME   BOXER NAME

VS

RUNNING TOTAL	POINTS DEDUCTED	ROUND SCORE	ROUND	ROUND SCORE	POINTS DEDUCTED	RUNNING TOTAL
			1			
			2			
			3			
			4			
			5			
			6			
			7			
			8			
			9			
			10			
			11			
			12			

TOTAL ⇒ [   ] [   ] **⇐ TOTAL**

DATE:

CITY:

VENUE:

REFEREE:

WEIGHT DIVISION:

TITLE:

NOTES:

WINNER:

OFFICIAL SCORES

JUDGE:	JUDGE:	JUDGE:

Boxing judges are trained to score matches using the following criteria:

1. Clean punching (power versus quantity)
2. Effective aggressiveness
3. Ring generalship
4. Defense

Source: Association of Boxing Commissions Regulatory Guidelines

FIGHTNEWS.COM® BOXING SCORECARD

BOXER NAME					BOXER NAME			DATE:

VS

RUNNING TOTAL	POINTS DEDUCTED	ROUND SCORE	ROUND	ROUND SCORE	POINTS DEDUCTED	RUNNING TOTAL
			1			
			2			
			3			
			4			
			5			
			6			
			7			
			8			
			9			
			10			
			11			
			12			

TOTAL ⇒ | | **⇐ TOTAL**

WINNER:

OFFICIAL SCORES

JUDGE:	JUDGE:	JUDGE:

DATE:

CITY:

VENUE:

REFEREE:

WEIGHT DIVISION:

TITLE:

NOTES:

Boxing judges are trained to score matches using the following criteria:

1. Clean punching (power versus quantity)
2. Effective aggressiveness
3. Ring generalship
4. Defense

Source: Association of Boxing Commissions Regulatory Guidelines

FIGHTNEWS.COM® BOXING SCORECARD

BOXER NAME				BOXER NAME			DATE:
		VS					CITY:

RUNNING TOTAL	POINTS DEDUCTED	ROUND SCORE	ROUND	ROUND SCORE	POINTS DEDUCTED	RUNNING TOTAL
			1			
			2			
			3			
			4			
			5			
			6			
			7			
			8			
			9			
			10			
			11			
			12			

VENUE:

REFEREE:

WEIGHT DIVISION:

TITLE:

NOTES:

TOTAL ⇒ [ ] [ ] **⇐ TOTAL**

WINNER:

OFFICIAL SCORES

JUDGE:	JUDGE:	JUDGE:

Boxing judges are trained to score matches using the following criteria:

1. Clean punching (power versus quantity)
2. Effective aggressiveness
3. Ring generalship
4. Defense

Source: Association of Boxing Commissions Regulatory Guidelines

FIGHTNEWS.COM® BOXING SCORECARD

BOXER NAME   BOXER NAME

VS

RUNNING TOTAL	POINTS DEDUCTED	ROUND SCORE	ROUND	ROUND SCORE	POINTS DEDUCTED	RUNNING TOTAL
			1			
			2			
			3			
			4			
			5			
			6			
			7			
			8			
			9			
			10			
			11			
			12			

TOTAL ⇒ [ ] [ ] **⇐ TOTAL**

DATE:

CITY:

VENUE:

REFEREE:

WEIGHT DIVISION:

TITLE:

NOTES:

WINNER:

OFFICIAL SCORES

JUDGE:	JUDGE:	JUDGE:

Boxing judges are trained to score matches using the following criteria:

1. Clean punching (power versus quantity)
2. Effective aggressiveness
3. Ring generalship
4. Defense

Source: Association of Boxing Commissions Regulatory Guidelines

FIGHTNEWS.COM® BOXING SCORECARD

BOXER NAME						BOXER NAME

VS

RUNNING TOTAL	POINTS DEDUCTED	ROUND SCORE	ROUND	ROUND SCORE	POINTS DEDUCTED	RUNNING TOTAL
			1			
			2			
			3			
			4			
			5			
			6			
			7			
			8			
			9			
			10			
			11			
			12			

TOTAL ⇒ [ ] [ ] **⇐ TOTAL**

WINNER:

OFFICIAL SCORES

JUDGE:	JUDGE:	JUDGE:

DATE:

CITY:

VENUE:

REFEREE:

WEIGHT DIVISION:

TITLE:

NOTES:

Boxing judges are trained to score matches using the following criteria:

1. Clean punching (power versus quantity)
2. Effective aggressiveness
3. Ring generalship
4. Defense

Source: Association of Boxing Commissions Regulatory Guidelines

FIGHTNEWS.COM® BOXING SCORECARD

BOXER NAME   BOXER NAME

VS

RUNNING TOTAL	POINTS DEDUCTED	ROUND SCORE	ROUND	ROUND SCORE	POINTS DEDUCTED	RUNNING TOTAL
			1			
			2			
			3			
			4			
			5			
			6			
			7			
			8			
			9			
			10			
			11			
			12			

TOTAL ⟹ [ ] [ ] **⟸ TOTAL**

WINNER:

OFFICIAL SCORES

JUDGE:	JUDGE:	JUDGE:

DATE:

CITY:

VENUE:

REFEREE:

WEIGHT DIVISION:

TITLE:

NOTES:

Boxing judges are trained to score matches using the following criteria:

1. Clean punching (power versus quantity)
2. Effective aggressiveness
3. Ring generalship
4. Defense

Source: Association of Boxing Commissions Regulatory Guidelines

FIGHTNEWS.COM® BOXING SCORECARD

BOXER NAME			VS		BOXER NAME		DATE:

RUNNING TOTAL	POINTS DEDUCTED	ROUND SCORE	ROUND	ROUND SCORE	POINTS DEDUCTED	RUNNING TOTAL
			1			
			2			
			3			
			4			
			5			
			6			
			7			
			8			
			9			
			10			
			11			
			12			

TOTAL ⇒ [ ] [ ] **⇐ TOTAL**

DATE:

CITY:

VENUE:

REFEREE:

WEIGHT DIVISION:

TITLE:

NOTES:

WINNER:

OFFICIAL SCORES

JUDGE:	JUDGE:	JUDGE:

Boxing judges are trained to score matches using the following criteria:

1. Clean punching (power versus quantity)
2. Effective aggressiveness
3. Ring generalship
4. Defense

Source: Association of Boxing Commissions Regulatory Guidelines

FIGHTNEWS.COM® BOXING SCORECARD

BOXER NAME							BOXER NAME	DATE:

VS

RUNNING TOTAL	POINTS DEDUCTED	ROUND SCORE	ROUND	ROUND SCORE	POINTS DEDUCTED	RUNNING TOTAL
			1			
			2			
			3			
			4			
			5			
			6			
			7			
			8			
			9			
			10			
			11			
			12			

TOTAL ⇒ [ ] [ ] **⇐ TOTAL**

WINNER:

OFFICIAL SCORES

JUDGE:	JUDGE:	JUDGE:

DATE:

CITY:

VENUE:

REFEREE:

WEIGHT DIVISION:

TITLE:

NOTES:

Boxing judges are trained to score matches using the following criteria:

1. Clean punching (power versus quantity)
2. Effective aggressiveness
3. Ring generalship
4. Defense

Source: Association of Boxing Commissions Regulatory Guidelines

FIGHTNEWS.COM® BOXING SCORECARD

BOXER NAME   BOXER NAME

VS

RUNNING TOTAL	POINTS DEDUCTED	ROUND SCORE	ROUND	ROUND SCORE	POINTS DEDUCTED	RUNNING TOTAL
			1			
			2			
			3			
			4			
			5			
			6			
			7			
			8			
			9			
			10			
			11			
			12			

TOTAL ⇒ | | **⇐ TOTAL**

WINNER:

OFFICIAL SCORES

JUDGE:	JUDGE:	JUDGE:

DATE:

CITY:

VENUE:

REFEREE:

WEIGHT DIVISION:

TITLE:

NOTES:

Boxing judges are trained to score matches using the following criteria:

1. Clean punching (power versus quantity)
2. Effective aggressiveness
3. Ring generalship
4. Defense

Source: Association of Boxing Commissions Regulatory Guidelines

FIGHTNEWS.COM® BOXING SCORECARD

BOXER NAME			VS		BOXER NAME	

DATE:

CITY:

VENUE:

REFEREE:

WEIGHT DIVISION:

TITLE:

NOTES:

RUNNING TOTAL	POINTS DEDUCTED	ROUND SCORE	ROUND	ROUND SCORE	POINTS DEDUCTED	RUNNING TOTAL
			1			
			2			
			3			
			4			
			5			
			6			
			7			
			8			
			9			
			10			
			11			
			12			

TOTAL ⇒ [　　] [　　] **⇐ TOTAL**

WINNER:

OFFICIAL SCORES

JUDGE:	JUDGE:	JUDGE:

Boxing judges are trained to score matches using the following criteria:

1. Clean punching (power versus quantity)
2. Effective aggressiveness
3. Ring generalship
4. Defense

Source: Association of Boxing Commissions Regulatory Guidelines

FIGHTNEWS.COM® BOXING SCORECARD

	BOXER NAME				BOXER NAME		

VS

RUNNING TOTAL	POINTS DEDUCTED	ROUND SCORE	ROUND	ROUND SCORE	POINTS DEDUCTED	RUNNING TOTAL
			1			
			2			
			3			
			4			
			5			
			6			
			7			
			8			
			9			
			10			
			11			
			12			

TOTAL ⇒ [   ] [   ] **⇐ TOTAL**

WINNER:

OFFICIAL SCORES

JUDGE:	JUDGE:	JUDGE:

DATE:

CITY:

VENUE:

REFEREE:

WEIGHT DIVISION:

TITLE:

NOTES:

Boxing judges are trained to score matches using the following criteria:

1. Clean punching (power versus quantity)
2. Effective aggressiveness
3. Ring generalship
4. Defense

Source: Association of Boxing Commissions Regulatory Guidelines

FIGHTNEWS.COM® BOXING SCORECARD

BOXER NAME			VS		BOXER NAME		DATE:

RUNNING TOTAL	POINTS DEDUCTED	ROUND SCORE	ROUND	ROUND SCORE	POINTS DEDUCTED	RUNNING TOTAL
			1			
			2			
			3			
			4			
			5			
			6			
			7			
			8			
			9			
			10			
			11			
			12			

TOTAL ⇒ [ ] [ ] **⇐ TOTAL**

DATE:

CITY:

VENUE:

REFEREE:

WEIGHT DIVISION:

TITLE:

NOTES:

WINNER:

OFFICIAL SCORES

JUDGE:	JUDGE:	JUDGE:

Boxing judges are trained to score matches using the following criteria:

1. Clean punching (power versus quantity)
2. Effective aggressiveness
3. Ring generalship
4. Defense

Source: Association of Boxing Commissions Regulatory Guidelines

FIGHTNEWS.COM® BOXING SCORECARD

BOXER NAME		BOXER NAME	DATE:

VS

RUNNING TOTAL	POINTS DEDUCTED	ROUND SCORE	ROUND	ROUND SCORE	POINTS DEDUCTED	RUNNING TOTAL
			1			
			2			
			3			
			4			
			5			
			6			
			7			
			8			
			9			
			10			
			11			
			12			

TOTAL ⇒ [   ] [   ] **⇐ TOTAL**

CITY:

VENUE:

REFEREE:

WEIGHT DIVISION:

TITLE:

NOTES:

WINNER:

OFFICIAL SCORES

JUDGE:	JUDGE:	JUDGE:

Boxing judges are trained to score matches using the following criteria:

1. Clean punching (power versus quantity)
2. Effective aggressiveness
3. Ring generalship
4. Defense

Source: Association of Boxing Commissions Regulatory Guidelines

FIGHTNEWS.COM® BOXING SCORECARD

BOXER NAME					BOXER NAME			DATE:
			VS					

RUNNING TOTAL	POINTS DEDUCTED	ROUND SCORE	ROUND	ROUND SCORE	POINTS DEDUCTED	RUNNING TOTAL
			1			
			2			
			3			
			4			
			5			
			6			
			7			
			8			
			9			
			10			
			11			
			12			

TOTAL ⇒ | | **⇐ TOTAL**

DATE:

CITY:

VENUE:

REFEREE:

WEIGHT DIVISION:

TITLE:

NOTES:

WINNER:

OFFICIAL SCORES

JUDGE:	JUDGE:	JUDGE:

Boxing judges are trained to score matches using the following criteria:

1. Clean punching (power versus quantity)
2. Effective aggressiveness
3. Ring generalship
4. Defense

Source: Association of Boxing Commissions Regulatory Guidelines

FIGHTNEWS.COM® BOXING SCORECARD

BOXER NAME						BOXER NAME	
			VS				

RUNNING TOTAL	POINTS DEDUCTED	ROUND SCORE	ROUND	ROUND SCORE	POINTS DEDUCTED	RUNNING TOTAL
			1			
			2			
			3			
			4			
			5			
			6			
			7			
			8			
			9			
			10			
			11			
			12			

TOTAL ⇒ | | ⇐ **TOTAL**

WINNER:

OFFICIAL SCORES

JUDGE:	JUDGE:	JUDGE:

DATE:

CITY:

VENUE:

REFEREE:

WEIGHT DIVISION:

TITLE:

NOTES:

Boxing judges are trained to score matches using the following criteria:

1. Clean punching (power versus quantity)
2. Effective aggressiveness
3. Ring generalship
4. Defense

Source: Association of Boxing Commissions Regulatory Guidelines

FIGHTNEWS.COM® BOXING SCORECARD

BOXER NAME						BOXER NAME	

VS

RUNNING TOTAL	POINTS DEDUCTED	ROUND SCORE	ROUND	ROUND SCORE	POINTS DEDUCTED	RUNNING TOTAL
			1			
			2			
			3			
			4			
			5			
			6			
			7			
			8			
			9			
			10			
			11			
			12			

TOTAL ⇒ [   ] [   ] **⇐ TOTAL**

WINNER:

OFFICIAL SCORES

JUDGE:	JUDGE:	JUDGE:

DATE:

CITY:

VENUE:

REFEREE:

WEIGHT DIVISION:

TITLE:

NOTES:

Boxing judges are trained to score matches using the following criteria:

1. Clean punching (power versus quantity)
2. Effective aggressiveness
3. Ring generalship
4. Defense

Source: Association of Boxing Commissions Regulatory Guidelines

FIGHTNEWS.COM® BOXING SCORECARD

BOXER NAME   VS   BOXER NAME

RUNNING TOTAL	POINTS DEDUCTED	ROUND SCORE	ROUND	ROUND SCORE	POINTS DEDUCTED	RUNNING TOTAL
			1			
			2			
			3			
			4			
			5			
			6			
			7			
			8			
			9			
			10			
			11			
			12			

TOTAL ⇒ [ ]   [ ] **⇐ TOTAL**

WINNER:

OFFICIAL SCORES

JUDGE:	JUDGE:	JUDGE:

DATE:

CITY:

VENUE:

REFEREE:

WEIGHT DIVISION:

TITLE:

NOTES:

Boxing judges are trained to score matches using the following criteria:

1. Clean punching (power versus quantity)
2. Effective aggressiveness
3. Ring generalship
4. Defense

Source: Association of Boxing Commissions Regulatory Guidelines

FIGHTNEWS.COM® BOXING SCORECARD

BOXER NAME						BOXER NAME	
			VS				

RUNNING TOTAL	POINTS DEDUCTED	ROUND SCORE	ROUND	ROUND SCORE	POINTS DEDUCTED	RUNNING TOTAL
			1			
			2			
			3			
			4			
			5			
			6			
			7			
			8			
			9			
			10			
			11			
			12			

TOTAL ⇒ [ ] [ ] ⇐ **TOTAL**

WINNER:

OFFICIAL SCORES

JUDGE:	JUDGE:	JUDGE:

DATE:

CITY:

VENUE:

REFEREE:

WEIGHT DIVISION:

TITLE:

NOTES:

Boxing judges are trained to score matches using the following criteria:

1. Clean punching (power versus quantity)
2. Effective aggressiveness
3. Ring generalship
4. Defense

Source: Association of Boxing Commissions Regulatory Guidelines

FIGHTNEWS.COM® BOXING SCORECARD

BOXER NAME				BOXER NAME			DATE:

VS

RUNNING TOTAL	POINTS DEDUCTED	ROUND SCORE	ROUND	ROUND SCORE	POINTS DEDUCTED	RUNNING TOTAL
			1			
			2			
			3			
			4			
			5			
			6			
			7			
			8			
			9			
			10			
			11			
			12			

TOTAL ⟹   **⟸ TOTAL**

DATE:

CITY:

VENUE:

REFEREE:

WEIGHT DIVISION:

TITLE:

NOTES:

WINNER:

OFFICIAL SCORES

JUDGE:	JUDGE:	JUDGE:

Boxing judges are trained to score matches using the following criteria:

1. Clean punching (power versus quantity)
2. Effective aggressiveness
3. Ring generalship
4. Defense

Source: Association of Boxing Commissions Regulatory Guidelines

FIGHTNEWS.COM® BOXING SCORECARD

BOXER NAME   BOXER NAME

VS

RUNNING TOTAL	POINTS DEDUCTED	ROUND SCORE	ROUND	ROUND SCORE	POINTS DEDUCTED	RUNNING TOTAL
			1			
			2			
			3			
			4			
			5			
			6			
			7			
			8			
			9			
			10			
			11			
			12			

TOTAL ⇒   **⇐ TOTAL**

WINNER:

OFFICIAL SCORES

JUDGE: JUDGE: JUDGE:

DATE:

CITY:

VENUE:

REFEREE:

WEIGHT DIVISION:

TITLE:

NOTES:

Boxing judges are trained to score matches using the following criteria:

1. Clean punching (power versus quantity)
2. Effective aggressiveness
3. Ring generalship
4. Defense

Source: Association of Boxing Commissions Regulatory Guidelines

FIGHTNEWS.COM® BOXING SCORECARD

BOXER NAME   BOXER NAME

<u>VS</u>

RUNNING TOTAL	POINTS DEDUCTED	ROUND SCORE	ROUND	ROUND SCORE	POINTS DEDUCTED	RUNNING TOTAL
			1			
			2			
			3			
			4			
			5			
			6			
			7			
			8			
			9			
			10			
			11			
			12			

TOTAL ⇒ [　　] [　　] **⇐ TOTAL**

DATE:
CITY:
VENUE:
REFEREE:
WEIGHT DIVISION:
TITLE:
NOTES:

WINNER:

OFFICIAL SCORES

JUDGE:	JUDGE:	JUDGE:

Boxing judges are trained to score matches using the following criteria:

1. Clean punching (power versus quantity)
2. Effective aggressiveness
3. Ring generalship
4. Defense

Source: Association of Boxing Commissions Regulatory Guidelines

FIGHTNEWS.COM® BOXING SCORECARD

| BOXER NAME | | | | BOXER NAME | | | DATE: |
| | | | | | | | |

VS

RUNNING TOTAL	POINTS DEDUCTED	ROUND SCORE	ROUND	ROUND SCORE	POINTS DEDUCTED	RUNNING TOTAL
			1			
			2			
			3			
			4			
			5			
			6			
			7			
			8			
			9			
			10			
			11			
			12			

TOTAL ⇒ | | ⇐ **TOTAL**

WINNER:

OFFICIAL SCORES

JUDGE:	JUDGE:	JUDGE:

DATE:

CITY:

VENUE:

REFEREE:

WEIGHT DIVISION:

TITLE:

NOTES:

Boxing judges are trained to score matches using the following criteria:

1. Clean punching (power versus quantity)
2. Effective aggressiveness
3. Ring generalship
4. Defense

Source: Association of Boxing Commissions Regulatory Guidelines

FIGHTNEWS.COM® BOXING SCORECARD

BOXER NAME			VS		BOXER NAME			DATE:

RUNNING TOTAL	POINTS DEDUCTED	ROUND SCORE	ROUND	ROUND SCORE	POINTS DEDUCTED	RUNNING TOTAL
			1			
			2			
			3			
			4			
			5			
			6			
			7			
			8			
			9			
			10			
			11			
			12			

TOTAL ⇒ [ ] [ ] ⇐ **TOTAL**

DATE:

CITY:

VENUE:

REFEREE:

WEIGHT DIVISION:

TITLE:

NOTES:

WINNER:

OFFICIAL SCORES

JUDGE:	JUDGE:	JUDGE:

Boxing judges are trained to score matches using the following criteria:

1. Clean punching (power versus quantity)
2. Effective aggressiveness
3. Ring generalship
4. Defense

Source: Association of Boxing Commissions Regulatory Guidelines

FIGHTNEWS.COM® BOXING SCORECARD

BOXER NAME			VS		BOXER NAME		DATE:

RUNNING TOTAL	POINTS DEDUCTED	ROUND SCORE	ROUND	ROUND SCORE	POINTS DEDUCTED	RUNNING TOTAL
			1			
			2			
			3			
			4			
			5			
			6			
			7			
			8			
			9			
			10			
			11			
			12			

TOTAL ⇒ | | **⇐ TOTAL**

DATE:

CITY:

VENUE:

REFEREE:

WEIGHT DIVISION:

TITLE:

NOTES:

WINNER:

OFFICIAL SCORES

JUDGE:	JUDGE:	JUDGE:

Boxing judges are trained to score matches using the following criteria:

1. Clean punching (power versus quantity)
2. Effective aggressiveness
3. Ring generalship
4. Defense

Source: Association of Boxing Commissions Regulatory Guidelines

FIGHTNEWS.COM® BOXING SCORECARD

BOXER NAME				BOXER NAME		
			VS			
RUNNING TOTAL	POINTS DEDUCTED	ROUND SCORE	ROUND	ROUND SCORE	POINTS DEDUCTED	RUNNING TOTAL
			1			
			2			
			3			
			4			
			5			
			6			
			7			
			8			
			9			
			10			
			11			
			12			

TOTAL ⇒ [   ] [   ] **⇐ TOTAL**

WINNER:

OFFICIAL SCORES

JUDGE:	JUDGE:	JUDGE:

DATE:

CITY:

VENUE:

REFEREE:

WEIGHT DIVISION:

TITLE:

NOTES:

Boxing judges are trained to score matches using the following criteria:

1. Clean punching (power versus quantity)
2. Effective aggressiveness
3. Ring generalship
4. Defense

Source: Association of Boxing Commissions Regulatory Guidelines

FIGHTNEWS.COM® BOXING SCORECARD

BOXER NAME   BOXER NAME

VS

RUNNING TOTAL	POINTS DEDUCTED	ROUND SCORE	ROUND	ROUND SCORE	POINTS DEDUCTED	RUNNING TOTAL
			1			
			2			
			3			
			4			
			5			
			6			
			7			
			8			
			9			
			10			
			11			
			12			

TOTAL ⇒ [ ]   [ ] **⇐ TOTAL**

WINNER:

OFFICIAL SCORES

JUDGE:	JUDGE:	JUDGE:

DATE:

CITY:

VENUE:

REFEREE:

WEIGHT DIVISION:

TITLE:

NOTES:

Boxing judges are trained to score matches using the following criteria:

1. Clean punching (power versus quantity)
2. Effective aggressiveness
3. Ring generalship
4. Defense

Source: Association of Boxing Commissions Regulatory Guidelines

Congratulations!

You have scored more than 100 fights.

Don't stop now!

Get another **Fightnews.com® Scorebook**
at Amazon.com!

Made in the USA
Monee, IL
07 May 2020